WHITMAN COLLEGE LIBRARY

WITHDRAWN BY
WHITMAN COLLEGE LIBRARY

ETHNICITY
AND ETHNIC GROUP PERSISTENCE
IN AN ACADIAN VILLAGE
IN MARITIME CANADA

Immigrant Communities & Ethnic Minorities in the United States & Canada: 4
[ISSN 0749-5951]

ETHNICITY AND ETHNIC GROUP PERSISTENCE IN AN ACADIAN VILLAGE IN MARITIME CANADA

Nanciellen Davis

AMS PRESS
NEW YORK

Library of Congress Cataloging in Publication Data
Davis, Nanciellen.
 Ethnicity and Ethnic Group Persistence in an Acadian Village in Maritime Canada.

 (Immigrant Communities & Ethnic Minorities in the United States & Canada, ISSN 0749–5951; 4)
  Bibliography: p.
  Includes index.
  1. French-Canadians—New Brunswick—Sainte-Marie-sur-Mer—Ethnic identity. 2. Sainte-Marie-sur-Mer (N.B.)—Ethnic relations. I. Title. II. Series.
 F1044.5.S2D38 1985 305.8'114'071512 83-45352
 ISBN 0-404-19405-2

COPYRIGHT © 1985 by AMS PRESS, INC.
All rights reserved

Manufactured in the United States of America

To my mother and in memory
of my father

CONTENTS

Foreword		ix
Preface		xi
Chapter One	Canadian Dualism and the Acadian Dilemma	1
Chapter Two	Ethnic Relations, Persistence, and Assimilation: Approaches to Acadian Studies	19
Chapter Three	The Region	38
Chapter Four	The Village	55
Chapter Five	Making a Living	66
Chapter Six	Patterning Continuity: Kinship	94
Chapter Seven	Structuring Interaction: Within the Parish	124
Chapter Eight	Structuring Interaction: The Parish and Beyond	144
Chapter Nine	Ethnic Persistence, Ethnicity, and Conflict	158
Chapter Ten	Postscript	176
Maps		188
Appendix		194
Notes		203
Bibliography		209
Index		223

TABLES

I	Distribution of Population with French as a Mother Tongue in the Maritime Provinces (Counties Having 10 Percent or More French Language Population), 1971 and 1981	13
II	Occupations of Villagers, Ste. Marie-sur-Mer	67
III	Origin of Heads of Households, Residence in Ste. Marie, and Means of Household Land Acquisition	113

MAPS

1	Gloucester County, Northeastern New Brunswick, Showing Shippegan (Lameque) Island and Ste. Marie-sur-Mer	189
2	New Brunswick: Cities, Counties, Main Highways, and Major Rivers	191
3	Southeastern Part of Lameque Island, Showing Ste. Marie-sur-Mer and Neighboring Villages	193

FOREWORD

Most of the material presented here remains essentially as it was written in 1974. That is not to deny that events have occurred which have affected language use and French-English relations in Canada. In additions to the Notes of Chapter One, I mention a few of these events, and I update relevant census information as well. Also it does not deny that changes have occurred in the life style of Acadians in northeastern New Brunswick, particularly in what is now called the Acadian Peninsula wherein the village described is located. In Chapter Ten I indicate some of those changes, as well as more general points regarding the position of the francophone population in the province today.

The original study recorded something of what a people experience who live in two worlds: a daily lived-in world in which language use and ethnicity are not contentious and a larger world in which minority status, determined by mother tongue and ethnic origin, remains an important, though not immediately present, reality. That situation continues today. The study also recorded aspects of maritime village life, some of which have since changed. With the early 1970s as the "ethnographic present," the study provides a baseline against which the results of future studies could be compared.

In recent years my research has shifted to another area in eastern New Brunswick as it was during the nineteenth century. This ethnohistorical study is of an area where the numbers of Acadians and Anglo-Canadians were relatively balanced. Because of this change in my research interests, I do not anticipate conducting further research in the Shippegan area.

Nevertheless, my appreciation of the area remains unchanged. On my most recent visit to the Acadian Peninsula, in the fall of 1983, I found again those things which I had earlier grown to prize--the inescapable ocean and sky, for in this essentially flat land only fog or blinding snow can obliterate their powerful presence; the smell of sea and fish; the activity at wharves as last catches are brought in and boats hauled up for the winter; and the warmth, generosity, and tenacity of the people. I hope some of that sense of the people and place are conveyed in the pages that follow.

Nanciellen Davis
Halifax, Nova Scotia
July, 1984

PREFACE

My experience on Lameque Island began in the spring of 1971 when my husband and I visited the area so that I could better consider the possibilities of doing fieldwork there.[1] At that time, we were mistaken for honeymooners, for, a local woman reasoned, who else would come there to spend a weekend during a time of year in which snow remains deep, temperatures cold, and activity best confined to the indoors? Beginning with that first weekend, we have spent many happy days in the area and have received more warmth and cooperation than could have been expected, especially as our variously purported roles--honeymooners, tourists, government spies, students--have continued to be less than clear to many local people.

Northeastern New Brunswick is an area heavily populated by French-speaking Acadians, about whom little has been written anthropologically. A theoretical interest in other island communities, specifically islands in the Caribbean region, as well as an interest in filling some of the substantive gaps in anthropological knowledge on New Brunswick Acadians had initially led me to consider fieldwork on Lameque Island. Ultimately, selection of the particular village on the island in which this study was done came about for pragmatic reasons--a village was chosen in which housing facilities were immediately available. Villagers of Ste. Marie-sur-Mer later told me that the accidental choice of their village was a very fortunate thing for me; elsewhere on the island, they said, inhabitants of other villages would not have been as friendly and helpful as were those of Ste. Marie. Though area residents with whom I had contact were generally cooperative and cordial, I have never had occasion to regret the selection of Ste. Marie as the particular village in which this study was conducted. Nevertheless, it should be noted that the ultimate focus which the study acquired reflects an ex post facto decision; recognition of this focus prior to choosing a study site would have caused me to question the choice of Ste. Marie.

Specifically, the study focuses on the ethnic persistence of villagers in Ste. Marie-sur-Mer; I contend that the cultural processes which bring together villagers in reinforcement of bonds and which minimize contacts between villagers and Anglo-Canadians are responsible for this persistence. However, only a small population of Anglo-Canadians live in close proximity to Ste. Marie, and the opportunities for interaction between the two groups can be understood as being limited for that reason, and, thus, my cultural explanation of how contacts are minimized is weakened. A stronger test of the structuring of contacts as an explanation of ethnic persistence would have resulted if the region selected for study had held relatively balanced numbers of the two groups, as is found in various areas in New Brunswick. Retrospective assessment of the fieldwork experience is apparently often full of such insights.

Since the spring of 1971, my husband and I have had continuing

PREFACE   xiii

contact with the Lameque area and its inhabitants. Residence in Ste. Marie was carried out from May til October in 1971, for three weeks in May 1972, and two weeks in May 1973. Several weekends have been spent in the village during winters over the course of two years. During weekend trips we have stayed in the homes of area residents; for the longer periods of residence we lived in a small chalet owned by a villager and located near the wharf from which the inshore fishery was conducted.

My husband, an Anglo-Canadian from northeastern New Brunswick, accompanied me in the field for much of the time. I consider his presence to have been helpful, both personally and professionally. His use of French was initially far superior to mine; his origins in the area were of use in establishing rapport with villagers. His Anglo-Irish forebears had been farmers-fishermen-woodsmen just as had been earlier residents of Ste. Marie; contacts between his kinsmen and residents of the Shippegan area had occurred for various economic reasons and these contacts were of use in making us somewhat less "strangers" to the area.

Much of the activities of village men within the fishery were realms from which I was excluded. My husband became the fisherman in the household and was eventually accepted as a regular member of one of the crews fishing inshore from Ste. Marie; he participated in lobster, cod, and herring fisheries and much of what I know regarding these fisheries is a result of his participation in them. His ability to get along with and to win the respect of local fishermen for being vaillant undoubtedly aided me and my work to a considerable degree.

During the course of fieldwork, traditional anthropological research techniques were employed, that is, participant-observation, conducting of informal interviews, giving of questionnaires, carrying out a household census, and collection of genealogies. Translators were sometimes used in contacts with monolingual francophones, especially early in the fieldwork period. Both French and English were used with bilinguals in the village.

In addition to the above research techniques, local church records were used in completing and verifying genealogies and in compiling information on vital statistics and ceremonial events. Local French newspapers, the daily L'Évangéline and the weeklies Le Voilier and La Tribune Chaleur, were subscribed to and read so that questions and events of wider import to francophones in New Brunswick, as well as of specific interest to those residents in the Shippegan area, could be followed. Since September of 1970, I have lived in southeastern New Brunswick, thirty miles from Moncton, an urban center containing a large number of Acadian people. Thus during these several years I have remained within the provincial milieu in which villagers of Ste. Marie live; the advantages of such residence are obvious in terms of being able to keep abreast of events of importance to villagers.

Fieldwork in a complex society like Canada is enriched by the availability of church and government records, censuses, and newspapers. However, there are also disadvantages in conducting fieldwork in a complex society. For example, many types of activities involving villagers take place beyond the village, parish, and island. In other words, villagers' activities do not neatly unfold outside the anthropologist's window. Villagers' mobility makes an investigator's participant-observation impossible in many realms of potential importance to understanding village life; even within the village, participant-observation is of a different order than that often described by anthropologists. Many domestic chores carried out by village women are today conducted largely by machines or appliances tucked away in the households' utility rooms. Women's daily work can be done quickly and solitarily in the morning. Much of my participation, then, was informal as I passed the time of day with women during afternoons before suppers were to be prepared. In recreational hours, much enjoyment for villagers comes from television viewing; participant-observation during a typical evening commonly took the form of watching television in someone's home, attending a softball game (we became avid supporters of St. Raphael Parish's balle-molle team), or perhaps just in walking about the village or neighborhood of residence. It seemed that an inordinate amount of time was spent in minimally productive pursuits, albeit pursuits by which our good intentions could be demonstrated.

An added difficulty in conducting fieldwork in a complex society is that there are many other outsiders whose activities resemble those of the anthropologist and these outsiders are interpreted by villagers to not have the villagers' best interests in mind. Social workers and government representatives are often reputed to be investigating villagers for purposes of denying them pensions, social assistance, and the like. Many villagers assumed I was a government spy who had similar goals in mind. Also, university researchers interested in folklore had visited the area several years prior to my arrival and the results of their research had not been well received locally. Villagers viewed the resulting published collection of folk tales as basically uncomplimentary, as, in effect, "making fun" of the villagers. In general, then, I had to convince villagers both of my harmlessness (i.e., I was not working for the government) and of my good intentions (i.e., I had no intention of presenting villagers in a light that would expose them to the ridicule of outsiders).

A story told my husband and me by one of the village men, M. Leger (a pseudonym, as are all the names of people referred to in the study), was interpreted by us to be a thinly veiled reminder of our obligations to villagers. The story involved an event that happened several decades earlier. As. M. Leger explained to us, over the course of several years contact a stranger had been accepted by the Leger family and treated as one of the family. The family, and M. Leger in particular, had been eventually repaid by the stranger's causing them great unhappiness and trouble; the stranger stole a large sum of money from the Leger household. The robbery was second in importance to the fact that the stranger had betrayed the trust and affection which the Leger family had generously given him. The point of M. Leger's story was clear. We hope never to betray the trust and affection so openly given to us by villagers of Ste. Marie.

Without the help and cooperation of villagers of Ste. Marie-sur-Mer, this study could not have been possible. Without the interest and warm generosity of a number of local people, our experience would have been much less rich and rewarding. <u>Merci</u> <u>bien</u> <u>à</u> <u>tous</u>.

                                                Nanciellen Davis Sealy
                                                Sackville, New Brunswick
                                                August, 1974

ACKNOWLEDGEMENTS

First, I wish to thank Milton Altschuler, Phillip J. C. Dark, Jerome S. Handler, Charles H. Lange, and Walter W. Taylor, some of whom served on my dissertation committee and all of whom gave generously of their time and experience as faculty members of the Department of Anthropology of Southern Illinois University, Carbondale. Jerome S. Handler deserves special recognition and appreciation. His patience, guidance, and encouragement over several years made the research project a valuable experience from which I could long benefit.

I would also like to thank the staff at the Mount Allison University Library, particularly Mrs. Margaret Wheeler, for their cheerful and ready assistance. Thanks also to Mrs. Elizabeth Rayworth who typed the manuscript with her usual good humor and care.

Appreciation also is expressed to Mount Saint Vincent University, which provided financial assistance for the preparation of the manuscript.

CANADIAN DUALISM AND THE ACADIAN DILEMMA

The purpose of this study is to account for the ethnic persistence of French-speaking Acadians in Ste. Marie-sur-Mer, a rural fishing village in New Brunswick, Canada. I contend that the processes which minimize contacts between villagers and Anglo-Canadians and which bring together villagers in interaction to strengthen their mutual bonds are responsible for this persistence. Thus I am concerned with what Barth has described as exclusion and incorporation, processes by which group boundaries persist in spite of long-term contact between members of separate ethnic groups (Barth 1969a:9-10).

In these first chapters I present background material against which processes of incorporation and exclusion are to be examined. Chapter One describes the relations between French Canadians and English Canadians and indicates the special status of one French-speaking minority, the Acadians. Chapter Two reviews the ways in which sociologists and anthropologists have described the Acadians' relations with Anglo-Canadians and the effects of these relations on Acadians; in this chapter I elaborate on the purpose of my study and the procedures I employ in examining these same topics examined by others interested in Acadian society. In Chapter Three I describe the region in which the village is found; Chapter Four is an overview of village life. Chapters Five through Eight describe how villagers' contacts with Anglo-Canadians are minimized and how villagers interact and thereby maintain the solidarity and integrity of the local Acadian community. Chapter Nine summarizes my findings and contains suggestions for future work focusing on ethnicity, persistence, and conflict. Chapter Ten constitutes a postscript, written ten years after the preceding chapters were completed.

DEFINITION OF TERMS

Assimilation can be defined as a process by which ethnic group[1] boundaries are broken down, with differences between the groups becoming blurred or indistinct (Borhek 1970:33); the term assimilation can also be used to refer to an end product of change, a state in which differences between once distinct ethnic groups are no longer discernible or when such differences are no longer the basis for ascription or self-ascription in such groups. In this study I use assimilation to refer to both a process and end product of change; the contexts in which the term appears make clear in which sense it is being used.

Various types of assimilation have been distinguished, each type being defined by the boundary maintaining mechanism that ceases to operate with the progressive assimilation of an ethnic group (Gordon 1964). According to Gordon's typology, "behavioral assimilation," or acculturation, refers to the erasing of culturally defined differences between two ethnic groups; this type of assimilation occurs most rapidly in contact situations, and involves cultural characteristics such as language, religious beliefs, folklore and art, habits of dress, eating, house construction; in other words, the verbal, philosophical, and material representations of a particular people (Gordon 1964:60-75 passim).

"Structural assimilation" is the process by which members of a particular ethnic group acquire full access to social positions in public or private sectors of the wider society; thus "ethnic origin is not a relevant attribute in the allocation of roles, rights, [and] facilities" (Vallee, Schwartz, and Darknell 1971:394). In other words, the members of two or more ethnic groups have come to share the same societal networks, groups, and institutions (Gordon 1964:60-75 passim).

Unless otherwise stated, in this study acculturation will refer to what Gordon has described as "behavioral assimilation" and assimilation will be used to refer to what has been termed "structural assimilation."

In the Canadian context the popular meaning of assimilation has generally been that of acculturation. Fears expressed by members of ethnic groups relate to the potential loss of a distinctive cultural heritage, specifically their language and religion. At the same time many members of ethnic groups aspire to structural assimilation. The occurrence of structural assimilation prior to, or in the absence of, cultural assimilation is not impossible, though it is apparently rare; Switzerland is often cited as one of the few countries in which this process has occurred.

Because of the importance attached to language rights and retention by French- and English-speaking Canadians, language deserves special consideration here. Languages in contact may themselves undergo changes in all subsystems; however, questions of purity of either French or English, and combatting anglicisms and francocisms in French and English, respectively, are of most interest to elitist elements in Canadian society. Among Canadians in general there is more interest in the change _of_ language than the change _in_ language. I will term as "language adoption" the process by which individuals increasingly employ a second language to the extent that the mother tongue is gradually excluded from daily use.

In Canada, "bilingualism" is a term which is used to characterize both individuals and institutions, such as provincial or municipal governments, hospitals, and schools. An individual is bilingual if he or she has relatively equal control of two languages; an institution is considered bilingual if services of that institution are provided in two languages (Royal Commission on Bilingualism and Biculturalism 1967:xxviii).

Following popular usage in Canada, I will use the term "anglophone" to refer to an individual whose mother tongue is English and "francophone" to refer to an individual for whom French is the first language. The term "Quebecker"[2] will refer to French-speaking residents of Quebec, and "French Canadian" will be used for French-speaking Canadians regardless of the province in which they live. The terms "English Canadian" and "Anglo-Canadian" will be used interchangeably to refer to English-speaking Canadians irrespective of their place of residence in Canada. The definition of "Acadian" will be taken up below.

BILINGUALISM AND BICULTURALISM IN CANADA

The sociocultural dualism reflected in the official Canadian recognition of two principle cultures and languages, French and English, distinguishes Canada from many other countries, including the United States. Fundamental differences between these two North American countries are reflected in the traditional description of the United States as a "melting pot," in which ethnic diversity becomes American homogeneity and the description of Canada as a "mosaic," in which people of various ethnic origins preserve their cultural differences. Both societal descriptions are symbolic and ideal, and, hence, have varying correlation with actual conditions. The "melting pot" image increasingly has been shown to be inaccurate in depicting the nature of identity and assimilation of ethnic minorities in the United States (Gordon 1964). In Canada the importance of an official policy to promote bilingualism and biculturalism has been to assure minority language rights in certain governmental domains and to allay the fears of French Canadians that acculturation was an unspoken, though nonetheless real, national goal.

Close to 27 percent of the Canadian population claim French as a mother tongue and francophones represent a numerical minority in all provinces except Quebec, where they constitute over 80 percent of the population. About 60 percent of the Canadian population are anglophones. Members of the 13 percent of the population claiming neither French nor English as a mother tongue usually adopt English as a second language, except in Quebec where they may adopt French (Royal Commission on Bilingualism and Biculturalism 1967:22-25).

Relatively few Canadians (about 12 percent) are bilingual in

French and English. Less than 5 percent of the anglophones speak French; about 30 percent of the francophones speak English. Quebec and New Brunswick contain the largest proportions of bilingual speakers, 25 and 19 percent respectively. Though Ontario has nearly a half-million bilinguals, they represent only 8 percent of that province's population (Royal Commission on Bilingualism and Biculturalism 1967:37-38).[3]

The present existence of francophones and anglophones in Canada stems from the long historical reshuffling of French and British colonial interests in North America. As early as 1604 the French had founded a settlement in what is presently the province of Nova Scotia; thus French colonists had been established in Canada for over 100 years when Britain gained lasting control of the eastern French colony of Acadia in 1713 and of the rest of New France, including the westerly colony of Canada, in 1763. With the fall of New France, some 65,000 French settlers in Canada became subjects of the English king.

Early acculturation and assimilation of the French were minimized by the concentration of the French population in largely rural areas, the firmness of French intentions to retain their language and religion, and an inability of the English to implement a consistent and comprehensive strategy to incorporate French and English in the same economic and political system. Each ethnic group contracted, as it were, into its own societal shell; face-to-face contacts were minimal and limited to a few contexts (Denton 1966).

Strategies of accommodation came to characterize much of French-English relations in Canada (Cook 1967; Wagley and Harris 1967).

Such accommodation is reflected in the nature of the Canadian federation, by which the province of Quebec, in which nearly four-fifths of all French Canadians live, retains powers to implement programs of special importance to Quebeckers, such as that of government-subsidized Catholic schools. Thus, all Canadians are integrated in a common political and economic framework but French Canadians and Anglo-Canadians are free to preserve and promote their cultural differences; this approach to ethnic diversity has caused Canada to be described as something of a unique plural society in which stability has been maintained in the face of cultural plurality (Broom 1960:881).

Accommodation and recognition of language rights have been customarily recognized in many areas in Canada, and officially endorsed at various levels in the government. However, the federal government recently considered it necessary to clarify and to put into law certain fundamental rights in order to head off what was described as an impending crisis over language rights. The Royal Commission on Bilingualism and Biculturalism, which conducted its investigations in the 1960s, noted that "while we do not underrate the role of custom or of incidental legislation in fleshing out the existing provisions of the Constitution, we must not forget that these rights are not entrenched and thus can be abrogated at will" (Royal Commission on Bilingualism and Biculturalism 1967:55).

The Royal Commission's recommendations that were incorporated into the Official Languages Act of 1969 were those that dealt with language rights in the federal government and administration, including courts and Parliament; that is, the population could use either French or English in dealing with departments, agencies, and institutions of the federal government. Federal government services were to be henceforth made available in both languages in areas in which the minority language group represented 10 percent or more of the population, in the federal capital of Ottawa, and at central or head offices of government agencies throughout Canada.

An Official Languages Act was also passed in New Brunswick in 1969. The act also insured that either French or English could be used in obtaining services from provincial government agencies, departments, and institutions (e.g., the legislature and courts). According to this act, the language of instruction in public, trade, and technical schools should be that of the students' mother tongue, unless the number of students speaking the minority language was too small to make that feasible; at that time, alternative arrangements would be made "in the spirit of the law." According to the provisions of both the federal and New Brunswick acts, government publications were to be printed in both languages and letters from the government written in whichever official language was requested.

Today, five years after the passage of the Official Languages Act, there remains among both French- and English-speakers considerable discontent and dissatisfaction regarding the two official languages.

Among Anglo-Canadians there are many who misunderstand the nature of the official languages legislation. Many believe the legislation means that all Canadians must become bilingual. As few anglophones are bilingual, regulations requiring bilingualism for those holding certain positions in the public service are interpreted as being discriminatory against English Canadians. Some English Canadians favor the repeal of recent legislation regarding bilingualism.

Among French Canadians, as among Anglo-Canadians, a range of opinions is held regarding linguistic and cultural rights. For some French Canadians the policy of encouraging bilingualism and biculturalism has relevance. For others, primarily in Quebec, such policies are no longer important; instead, French monolingualism in that province is promoted (Rioux 1969). Some Quebeckers hold the extreme position that the only option which will guarantee their language and cultural rights is the separation of Quebec from the rest of the country. One Quebec political party (Parti Quebecois) has as its avowed goal Quebec's independence through separation.[4] Though Canada has been relatively free of the kind of violence often accompanying so-called liberation movements, there have been some terrorist activities in recent years, including political kidnappings and the 1970 assassination of a Quebec provincial minister. Stability has been maintained, but the specter of Canada becoming another Northern Ireland is feared by some Canadians who believe legislation will not alter attitudes and fears, but perhaps will intensify them.[5]

Animosities between French and English involve a variety of issues with long histories; periodically, religion, education, language, political allegiance, and economic control have all been the basis for hostility between the two groups. Stereotypes each group holds about the other reflect both current and past conflicts:

> Perhaps the most derogatory view of the French Canadian is held by English Canadians in the western provinces and in Ontario, where many have never seen a French Canadian. In brief, to these extremists, a French

> Canadian is a backward peasant, a papist fanatic, a
> narrow-minded Catholic, and a medieval fossil clinging
> rigidly to an outmoded way of life. The province of
> Quebec is to them almost a "reservation" to be visited
> by tourists; Quebec's insistence upon the bicultural
> and bilingual basis for nationalism in Canada is but
> a bit of fantasy to be tolerated but not taken seriously;
> Canada is an English-speaking country and a part of the
> Empire. Many English Canadians, even in the province
> of Quebec, are convinced that Canada will eventually
> be English-speaking and English-Canadian in culture,
> and that the French-Canadian group will eventually
> disappear through acculturation and assimilation... .
>
> On the other hand, French-Canadian extremists
> still look upon <u>les anglais</u> as men with two countries--
> Great Britain and Canada... . The English Canadians are
> thought to be imperialist, much more interested in the
> welfare of the Empire than of Canada. Furthermore, the
> English Canadian is thought to be imperialist at home;
> he wishes only to exploit and to assimilate the French
> Canadians. Since the English Canadians are the majority
> in the federal Parliament, French Canadians suspect any
> federal laws or orders of being unfair and directed
> against French-Canadian interests. They think of the
> English Canadians as rich and powerful and in complete
> control of economic trusts which rule Quebec and the
> French Canadians. Personally, <u>les anglais</u> are considered
> to be materialists--practical men given to business--
> arrogant, proud of their "race", and lacking in con-
> sideration of others. The English are pictured as
> barbarians--more interested in dogs than in children,
> in sports than in religion, in money than in arts
> (Wagley and Harris 1967:184-85).

A climate of distrust, misunderstanding, and ignorance continues to characterize much of the relations between the two founding "races" of Canada today.[6]

There is little argument that Canada's particular dualistic character, which creates a sociocultural milieu quite richly and uniquely Canadian, also serves to create serious internal political problems. These difficulties have yet to be resolved and are suggested by many to represent essential problems to be solved if the federation is to continue in its present form.

BICULTURALISM, BILINGUALISM, AND ACADIANS

It has been suggested that there are many French Canadas, with the French in Manitoba, in Ontario, in Quebec, and in the Maritime Provinces possessing "certain basic interests in common" while having their own "different outlooks and problems" (Wade 1962:34). The assertion is undoubtedly true, though it must be noted that substantiation of regional differences and similarities has usually been approached in terms of history and demography (see, for example, Wade 1960). Regional variation in French Canada, including that associated with questions of bilingualism, acculturation, and assimilation, has received only limited attention from sociologists and anthropologists. Studies performed for the Royal Commission on Bilingualism and Biculturalism are exceptions which do address themselves to such topics (de la Garde 1966; Henripin 1966; Jolicoeur 1966) as do several recent publications dealing specifically with bilingualism and acculturation in Canada (Joy 1972; Lieberson 1970; Maheu 1970).[7] Increasing numbers of community or areal studies within Quebec (see, for example, Charest n.d.), and outside of Quebec, (Hebert and Vaillancourt 1971), will undoubtedly help provide a clearer picture of the social and cultural variation within French Canada.[8]

This study is concerned with inter-ethnic contacts and ethnic group persistence among French Canadians in one part of Canada. The regional population focused on comprises the 260,000 French Canadians who live in the Maritime Provinces, and most particularly those living in one village in northeastern New Brunswick.

Within the Maritime Provinces (New Brunswick, Nova Scotia, and

Prince Edward Island), francophones live in a variety of circumstances with reference to their numerical strength. In Prince Edward Island, francophones constitute only 7 percent and in Nova Scotia only 5 percent of the provincial populations. In only one county in Prince Edward Island and four in Nova Scotia do francophones constitute more than 10 percent of the population. In New Brunswick, where 34 percent of the province are francophone, seven counties have populations comprising more than 10 percent francophones, and three of those counties have proportions exceeding 80 percent (see Table I). The village described in this study is located in one of the latter counties, Gloucester County.

French Canadians in the Maritime Provinces are generally called Acadians. Not all francophones in the Maritimes are technically Acadian (descendants of seventeenth and eighteenth century French settlers of the colony of Acadia), but unless an individual is a recent immigrant to the area, or has access to extensive genealogical records, or has an identifiably Acadian surname, he himself may not know whether or not his ancestors were of that original colony. After the acquisition of New France by the British in 1763, Norman-French people, from what was later to be known as Quebec, entered the area which was to become the province of New Brunswick and together with Acadians created numerous new settlements there (Arsenault 1966:232-36). Residents of New Brunswick counties bordering on Quebec (especially those of Madawaska County) today have as many ties with Quebec as with the rest of francophone New Brunswick while they claim to be different from both Quebeckers and Acadians. Thus, not all those who are technically Acadian, as

Table I

Distribution of Population with French as a Mother Tongue
In the Maritime Provinces (Counties Having 10 Percent or
More French Language Population), 1971 and 1981

Province	County	Percent of Population with French as Mother Tongue	
		1971	1981
Prince Edward Island	Prince	14.3	11.4
Nova Scotia	Digby	38.0	33.5
	Inverness	18.7	16.1
	Richmond	40.5	32.6
	Yarmouth	31.5	26.8
New Brunswick	Gloucester	82.8	81.3
	Kent	81.4	78.1
	Madawaska	94.6	92.5
	Northumberland	25.8	25.9
	Restigouche	59.8	59.3
	Victoria	38.9	41.9
	Westmoreland	40.3	39.6

Source: Statistics Canada 1973 and 1984

defined above, may identify themselves as such (see de la Garde 1966:160).

Differences between Acadians and Quebeckers are both historical and contemporary. From the earliest days of French colonization, the French settlers did not make up a close-knit population. The settlers who came to the colonies of Canada (that part of New France west of the St. Lawrence River Valley) and Acadia (the easterly or maritime region of New France) were from different areas in France, with Acadians coming from the southwestern regions of Touraine, Poitou, Anjou, Saintonge, and Champagne (Arsenault 1966: 25), and Canadians coming from the northern and central areas of France (Wade 1962:36). While the two colonies were under French rule, they developed independently and were relatively isolated from each other. During this hundred years, or from 1610 to 1713, Acadians probably had more contact with New Englanders and the British than they did with Canadians (Wade 1962:36). Finally in the last fifty years of New France, or from 1713 to 1763, much of what had been Acadia was under British control, and, hence, relations between the two French populations were further restricted.

Acadians have had a long history of contact with English-speaking populations. Acadians learned early to adapt to political and economic circumstances which involved prolonged interaction with British and then with Anglo-Canadians. For many Canadians, contacts with British, other than those on the battlefield, were limited even after the fall of Canada (Denton 1966).

The mid-eighteenth century <u>grand dérangement</u> in which most Acadians were expelled from their homes, stripped of property and belongings, and deported to various regions in America and Europe, was an experience which further served to mark off Acadians as a special segment within French Canadians as a whole. The sufferings experienced by Acadians, many of whom were to be forever separated from family and friends, and the hardships stubbornly overcome by many who by land and sea made their way back to their homeland in Maritime Canada, created deep-seated bonds among Acadians and later among their descendants. Longfellow's immortalization of the Acadian grand dérangement in his poem Evangeline has been of further importance in creating a certain romantic image of an Acadian people; many English speakers know little else of Acadians, past or present, other than the description contained in that poem.

Today dialect differences readily distinguish Acadians from French-speakers in the rest of Canada (Brent 1971); these differences have developed from those originally held by settlers and because of the relative isolation in which the French Canadian populations have lived. A particular world view has been attributed to today's Acadians, one which stresses the importance of tradition, religion, family, and the uniqueness of Acadians who, for example, survived the grand dérangement because of spiritual strength and Divine intervention (Hughes, Tremblay, Rapoport, and Leighton 1960:140-161; Tremblay 1961). As far as I know, however, a systematic comparison of the world views of Acadians and other French Canadians has not been attempted. Although certain institutions within Acadian and French Canadian areas have similar importance, e.g., the ecclesiastical parish is the major local-level unit of social organization in rural areas, differences at a cultural level, in terms of the "ideational system [comprising] categories, recipes, and rules for dealing with experience" (Keesing and Keesing 1971:348) may exist between the various groups, reflecting different historical experiences and contemporary societal arrangements.

Readily substantiated differences between Acadians and Quebeckers rest in the standards of living of the two groups. Acadians in the Maritimes have less formal education, less income and the power associated with it, less access to managerial positions and skilled industrial jobs than do French Canadians in Quebec. Such disparities are lessening, though they still remain valid indicators of differences between the two French populations (Wade 1962).[9]

Similarly, before recent legislation provided for language minority rights, Acadians had to rely on custom and cooperation for many of the rights they enjoyed. French Canadians in Quebec have had considerable political power as a strong majority in an important province, while Acadians in Nova Scotia, Prince Edward Island, and New Brunswick have constituted minorities in small, poor provinces. For example, Quebec members of the federal House of Commons presently number seventy-four, or about 28 percent of all the House seats; members from the three Maritime Provinces number only twenty-five, or about 9 percent of the seats in the House. In Quebec itself, protection and strengthening of French Canadian language and culture have long been established goals. In the Maritime Provinces, provincial attention to the needs and interests of the francophone minorities has been sporadic at best.

Finally, and most important in understanding that Acadians are a separate population within French Canada, is the fact that Acadians and Quebeckers see themselves as being different; each holds stereotypes about the other which are almost as disparaging as those jointly held about the Anglo-Canadians. Many Acadians consider Quebeckers political extremists and interpret their behavior towards Acadians as condescending, if not insulting. Many Quebeckers, on the other hand, seem to consider the poorer, less well-educated, and largely rural-dwelling Acadians as something of an embarrassment to French Canada. To those from Quebec, Acadians are culturally and linguistically a mixture, almost as much English as French. The Quebec government recently refused a grant to the company presenting the highly acclaimed Acadian dramatic monologue La Sagouine; the work includes the use of language typical of Acadian speech, which was not considered acceptable French by Quebec standards.

Just as past and present conditions have served to differentiate Acadians and Quebeckers, so too have different futures been predicted for the two groups. With the exception of those Acadians living in northern and eastern New Brunswick counties (where the percentages of francophones range between 26 and 95 percent), English language adoption has been forecast as an ultimate reality for francophones in the Maritime Provinces. Demographic factors, including a drop in the Acadian birth rate and continued outmigration of Acadians to Anglo-dominated urban areas, have been predicted to result in the disappearance of francophone population pockets. So-called "bilingual belts," such as northern and eastern New Brunswick, are predicted to remain, though perhaps narrowing, while the boundaries of monolingual regions on either side harden (Joy 1972; see also Lieberson 1970; Maheu 1970).[10]

A future in which a separate Acadian identity can be maintained is considered uncertain by many who forecast that many Acadians will be under increasing pressure either to identify with Quebeckers or be absorbed by Anglo-Canadians. This is a familiar problem for Acadians who, over the last 350 years, have been something of pawns caught between the two groups; familiarity does not make the position any more comfortable, however, nor solutions any more accessible.

In this chapter I have indicated that relations between French Canadians and English Canadians have suffered from misunderstanding and mistrust; one of the sources of contention has been that regarding the future of French Canadians as a linguistically distinct group. Acadians share the concern of all French Canadians regarding this issue, however they are in a generally more difficult position in attempting to resist acculturation than are residents of Quebec. In the next chapter I review the ways in which the Acadians' relations with Anglo-Canadians have been described in the literature and indicate my purpose and procedures in examining this same topic.

ETHNIC RELATIONS, PERSISTENCE, AND ACCULTURATION:
APPROACHES TO ACADIAN STUDIES

There are several Acadian societies in the Maritime Provinces, each experiencing different situations of inter-ethnic group contact, and thus each facing slightly different problems in maintaining their numbers and identity. As indicated below, however, relatively little is known about those contact situations; most commonly researchers focus on the results of contact, as reflected in census information on language use, and thus the processes of acculturation or of ethnic group maintenance remain little understood.

STUDIES OF CONTEMPORARY ACADIANS

Interest in Acadian history has never lagged.[1] Extensive historical research has dealt with topics such as the eighteenth century grand dérangement and the renaissance acadienne in the latter part of the nineteenth century. In comparison, studies regarding present-day Acadian society have been much less numerous. This may, in part, reflect the differences in the development of history and sociology-anthropology as disciplines within universities of the Maritime Provinces.

Until recently the sociological and anthropological publications dealing with immigrant groups in Newfoundland, New Brunswick, Nova Scotia, and Prince Edward Island have been limited in number; in recent years, however, there has been an outpouring of materials on immigrant groups in Newfoundland, specifically Anglo-Canadian residents of the coastal outports (e.g., Faris 1966; Firestone 1967; Szwed 1966; Wadel 1969); materials on Blacks in Nova Scotia have also appeared (e.g., Whitten, Jr. 1970; Clark 1971; Henry 1973).

In anthropological studies of Canadian populations, publications on immigrant groups have undoubtedly been more limited than those dealing with aboriginal populations. With a few notable exceptions, such as Horace Miner's thirty-five year old study of St. Denis, Quebec (Miner 1967), anthropologists have only in recent years combined a traditional interest in native groups with an interest in less exotic populations in Canada and North America as a whole. Acadians, as one of these less exotic populations, have received relatively little attention. Almost all of the anthropological publications dealing with Acadians are the work of one man, Marc-Adélard Tremblay.

I will not attempt a detailed review of the types of studies which have been done on twentieth century Acadians. This literature contains: local histories which describe communities and locales where Acadians live (e.g., Ganong 1906; 1908); descriptive works devoted to the history and activities of patriotic, religious, or financial institutions in present-day communities, and devoted to the contribution made by particular families or individuals to the development of the community as a whole (e.g., Michaud 1955; Chiasson 1961); and studies of language and folklore (e.g., Dulong

1961; Massignon 1962; Savoie 1967; Brent 1971).[2] In addition a considerable amount of research has been done by, or submitted to, the government.

Several reports or briefs dealing with Acadians were submitted to the Royal Commission on Bilingualism and Biculturalism; these reports took the form of overviews of various topics, e.g., the history and contemporary situation of Acadians in Maritime Canada (Baudry 1966); a study of the acculturation of francophones in New Brunswick as reflected in the utilization of the French language in New Brunswick, i.e., an analysis of the contexts in which French is used by different segments of the francophone population (de la Garde 1966).

Various studies have also been done to provide background material for government agencies formulating socioeconomic development programs (see, for example, Community Improvement Corporation Planning Department 1968). Northeastern New Brunswick, officially designated as Gloucester County, Restigouche County, and Alnick Parish in Northumberland County, has been recognized as an area particularly hard-pressed economically and deserving of special government attention. As a result, two hundred million dollars have been earmarked for development projects in the area; federal funds from the ARDA and FRED agreements (Agricultural Rehabilitation and Development Act, 1962, and Rural Economic Development Act, 1966) have been allotted for various programs planned by the province.

Although the above kinds of research are of importance and value to Acadian studies in general, the research reports done for the Royal Commission on Bilingualism and Biculturalism deal most explicitly with the relations between Acadians and Anglo-Canadians,

and with the Acadians' position vis-à-vis Anglo-Canadians.[3] I will
focus the rest of this review of the literature on those studies
which deal with inter-ethnic group relations and contacts.

Researchers interested in contemporary Acadian society and the
relations between Acadians and Anglo-Canadians have generally concluded that Acadians have effectively resisted acculturation and
assimilation because of their physical and social isolation (see,
for example, Baudry 1966). Thus the maintenance of ethnic
boundaries and retention of Acadian ethnicity, or "sense of peoplehood" (Gordon 1964:24) is attributed to the absence of interaction
between the two ethnic groups. The socioeconomic position of
Acadians vis-à-vis their Anglo-Canadian neighbors remains a topic
for debate, as reflected in articles appearing in periodicals published by the Université de Moncton and Université de Laval.

These publications often present conflicting views of Acadian
society. Conflicting interpretations are particularly evident with
respect to the socioeconomic position of Acadians in relation to
that of Anglo-Canadians in New Brunswick, and the programs for
development and change which will enable Acadians to improve their
socioeconomic position.

In essence, the same data, namely statistical or census information assembled by the federal government, are employed to support
the conflicting interpretations. Cadieux, for example, argues that
Acadians in New Brunswick are no poorer than their Anglo-Canadian
neighbors and that the stardard of living for members of both groups
is about the same (Cadieux 1968). Cadieux compares counties within
New Brunswick to illustrate that individual French counties have no

exclusive claim to poverty. For example, Westmoreland County, with 43.7 percent of its residents being francophone, has roughly the same average family income for its non-agricultural population as does York County with a population containing only 6.2 percent francophones (i.e., $4,628 in Westmoreland, $4,523 in York); Queens and Gloucester Counties, with populations of 91.5 percent English and 85 percent French, respectively, also have roughly the same average family incomes for non-agricultural populations (i.e., $3,291 in Gloucester, $3,607 in Queens) (Cadieux 1968:46-47).

Other sociologists, however, suggest that Acadians are decidedly poorer than their Anglo-Canadian neighbors. These writers maintain that the predominantly French area, i.e., northern and eastern New Brunswick, is poorer than the predominantly English area, i.e., the south-southwestern part of the province. Counties are grouped as being English (two-thirds of the population is of English origin), French (two-thirds of the population is of French origin) or mixed (neither French nor English constitute a two-thirds majority) and comparative statements are made regarding the socioeconomic positions of residents in the three types of counties. An example of the kind of comparison that might be made is: the average family income in English counties of New Brunswick is $4,102; in mixed counties it is $3,995, and in French counties it is $3,513 (Baudry 1966:8). Thus, by grouping all counties according to ethnic composition, more discrepancy can be shown to exist between French and English in New Brunswick, than by comparing the situations found in selected individual counties.

Recommendations to improve the lot of Acadians depend on the

view held by researchers of the current Acadian position. For those
who see Acadians as simply being residents of a poor province,
development of the province as a whole is advocated (Cadieux 1968).
For those who see Acadians as the disadvantaged of the province,
radical change is needed to upset old relationships in which Anglo-
Canadians have exercised socioeconomic and political dominance over
Acadians. For Cadieux, the problems of Acadians are primarily
educational and economic; if the appropriate provincial institutions are upgraded, the standard of living and well-being of all
will improve. According to others, change must be ideological and
political as well as educational-economic (Even 1970; Hautecoeur
1971; Poulin 1972; Richard 1969).[4]

In these last mentioned works, socioeconomic disparities between
French and English are described as symptoms of an Acadian cultural
malaise, including issues of power and identity. In the traditional
societal framework in which Acadians have participated in New
Brunswick, they have been dominated both socioeconomically and
culturally; Acadians are represented as having been relatively
powerless. Acculturation has continued to take its toll among
Acadians and between 1961 and 1971 the proportion of the population
claiming French as a mother tongue has dropped in all three Maritime
Provinces: from 7 to 5 percent in Nova Scotia, from 12 to 7 percent
in Prince Edward Island, and from 38 to 34 percent in New Brunswick.
Moreover, the proposed Maritime Union of the three Maritime
Provinces would diminish the francophone minority in the region as
a whole, as compared to the minority position of Acadians in New
Brunswick today. Hence, Acadian identity is said to be threatened.

APPROACHES TO ACADIAN STUDIES					25

These sociologists describe the options open to Acadians as total acculturation to Anglo-Canadian culture, identification with Quebec (and, perhaps, even amalgamation with an independent Quebec), or the forging of a new Acadian identity which could contend with traditional Anglo-dominance so that Acadians could progress and develop in all sociocultural realms. Acculturation is not endorsed (Even 1970; Hautecoeur 1971; Poulin 1972; Richard 1969).

Thus, new leadership among Acadians, as maintained in the writings of these sociologists (one of whom has recently been elected president of the Société des Acadiens du Nouveau-Brunswick, the major nationalistic Acadian association in New Brunswick), has as its goal the survival of the Acadian people, the same goal of earlier leadership or the old elite of religious leaders, educators, and businessmen. However, the means for achieving this end have been altered; there has been a shift from a dependence on spiritual superiority and self-imposed isolation as a means to secular survival, to a dependence on economic development so that factors encouraging acculturation can be fought. For example, industrialization in northern New Brunswick is encouraged because not only will the development be presumably of financial benefit to local Acadians but also the Acadians will no longer be forced to emigrate in search of jobs to Anglo-dominated regions of southern New Brunswick and elsewhere (Poulin 1971).

Considered necessary in improving the position of Acadians is the uniting of all Acadians and the creation of a new image and identity for Acadians--a more forceful, assertive, perhaps militant, identity essential for coping with the social milieu. Various events in recent years (e.g., student strikes and sit-ins at the Université de Moncton, confrontation between francophone students and anglophone municipal administrators in Moncton, change in the policies of Acadian institutions, introduction of new Acadian leadership, the making of several consciousness-raising films dealing with Acadians) are interpreted by Richard (1969) and Poulin (1972) as attempts by at least a certain segment of Acadian society to create a new identity.

I suggest that the interpretation of these events is itself an "event"; this view of Acadian society by French Canadian sociologists is in itself a social fact to be examined. In effect, clearer boundaries are being identified as lying between francophones and anglophones in New Brunswick: Acadians are dominated (socially, culturally, and economically) by anglophones. Acadians are being encouraged to unite in common cause; such emphasis on group unity again draws attention to group boundaries. However, as a consequence of attempts to create a new Acadian identity, old boundaries between Acadians and Quebeckers are being weakened or encouraged to be weakened; certain Acadian cultural symbols (e.g., the Acadian flag, the theme or story of the grand dérangement) are symbolically destroyed and put aside by those seeking a new Acadian identity (Poulin 1972). All of these developments are of considerable interest in considering the future of Acadian identity in New Brunswick. They are of interest, as well, as strategies employed in aligning or realigning inter-ethnic group relations and in strengthening group boundaries.

Generally, anthropological studies of Acadians have focused on social institutions and groups, particularly kinship and kin groups, and changes within them; change has often been interpreted to be acculturative. Ethnic relations between Anglo-Canadians and Acadians have been approached in terms of individual contacts which affect Acadians adversely in that they are the ones who are changed by the contact as they become progressively more anglicized and less Acadian. Such change is seen to disrupt, if not destroy, the traditional social structure. Also, change or acculturation is viewed largely in terms of result, rather than process; cultural content within the Acadian community, rather than ongoing interethnic relations, has been of foremost interest.

Anthropological studies of Acadians have been limited both in number and in representativeness of Acadian society as a whole. Although five-sixths of all Acadians in the Maritime Provinces live in New Brunswick, no anthropological field studies had been made of Acadians in the province. Statements about Acadian society are based on information gained from studies of Nova Scotian Acadians who live in circumstances which are in some ways (demographic, economic, political) quite different from those known by many Acadians in New Brunswick. Although it has been traditional in anthropology for one community, or one segment of a population, to be offered as a microcosm of the larger society, the approach has become increasingly suspect, especially when applied to a highly industrialized and complex society such as Canada. Additional studies of Acadians in various social environments are sorely needed. For example, it is commonly stated that three distinct francophone populations are found in New Brunswick: that of the northwest

(including the residents of the self-proclaimed République de
Madawaska), that of the northeast, and that of the southeast
(Moncton and surrounding area). However, sociocultural differences
between the three regional populations have not yet been systematically explored.

One brief article dealing with New Brunswick Acadians has been
published (Rioux 1955/56), and this has been cited as substantiation for the cultural unity of Acadian society, for the sentiments
of New Brunswick Acadians listed in the article correspond to those
attributed to Acadians of l'Anse des Lavallée in Nova Scotia
(Tremblay 1961:249; 1962b:154). The correlation is of interest;
however, it must be noted that Rioux did not claim the sentiments
were those of all New Brunswick Acadians. Rioux researched his
article by culling publications and documents, especially those
materials written during the <u>renaissance</u> <u>acadienne</u>, for indications
of ideology espoused by those attempting to create a <u>conscience</u>
<u>nationale,</u> or sense of peoplehood (Rioux 1955/56:63). Many of
these materials were written by religious figures and educators
who were often writing what might properly be called instructive
and inspirational tracts on the glories and miseries of Acadians
past and present. These works probably had considerable importance
in instilling a certain world view in Acadians to whom their message
was directed; something of a self-fulfilling prophecy may have
been in operation, just as publications of certain present-day French
Canadian sociologists may be performing a similar role. However,
the correlation between ideology expressed by elitist authors during
the <u>renaissance</u> <u>acadienne</u> to Acadian "sentiments," or world view,

held by members of other segments of New Brunswick Acadian society, past or present, should not be assumed; the usually presumed correlation should be investigated further, rather than be accepted as fact.

One of the most important programs of social science research dealing with Maritime Canada was the Stirling County Study, conducted in Nova Scotia; the study included the Acadian community l'Anse des Lavallée. This study of l'Anse des Lavallée represents the first such work done by trained researchers in an Acadian community.

The Stirling County Study focused on "the possible effects of sociocultural factors on the origin, course, and outcome of psychiatric disorders" (Hughes, Tremblay, Rapoport, and Leighton 1960:1). Important research topics of the study were social change, assimilation, and acculturation; the communities studied were characterized by "disintegration" or "integration," according to such variables as "cultural confusion," "widespread secularization," "rapid and widespread social change" (Hughes, Tremblay, Rapoport, and Leighton 1960:4). The functional model in which the study was framed called for value consensus and cultural stability, if not resistance to change, as characteristics of the integrated community. The absence of such characteristics indicated disintegration or disorganization and was often associated with psychiatric disorders in community members.

This model has continued to characterize Tremblay's publications on Acadians and acculturation, and acculturation has been used as an indicator of disintegration of the social system (Tremblay 1961; 1962a).

In Tremblay's early articles, indications of acculturation are the loss of, or reduction in, the use of the French language, and the weakening of adherence to the Catholic faith among individual Acadians (Tremblay 1961; 1962a). One of the devices commonly employed by researchers to measure French Canadian acculturation involves examining the percentage of the population claiming French origin which also claims English as its mother tongue. For example, 57 percent of the population in Nova Scotia, 55 percent in Prince Edward Island, and 12 percent in New Brunswick who claim French origin, also claim English as a mother tongue (Royal Commission on Bilingualism and Biculturalism 1967:33). Though the accuracy of this measure of acculturation has been questioned (Joy 1972:137-38), it does remain as something of a valid indicator of the extent of French language loss by those of French origin in the Maritime Provinces.

Similarly, since Acadians are nearly always Roman Catholic, change in religious affiliation (i.e., an Acadian who no longer adheres to the Catholic faith) has been described by investigators as a sign of acculturation (Hughes, Tremblay, Rapoport, and Leighton 1960; Tremblay 1962a). Tremblay recognizes that, among Acadians, the weakening of adherence to the Catholic faith (e.g., infrequent attendance at Mass, infrequent reception of the sacraments of confession and communion, weak religious convictions) may result from the influences of an urban way of life, rather than from acculturative pressures, but he considers the distinction between the two types of influences difficult to ascertain (Tremblay 1962a:299).

More recently, Tremblay has expanded on the indicators of acculturation found among Acadians. Among areas in which acculturation is now seen to have taken place are in occupational patterns, social structure (familial and societal), and value orientations or "sentiments" (Tremblay 1966).

Factors which trigger and contribute to acculturation result from technological and economic change, e.g., today Acadians accept wage labor and work beyond the Acadian area, rather than remaining at home to engage in subsistence activities (Tremblay 1966:331-32). Also important in encouraging acculturation among Nova Scotian Acadians are isolation from other French-speaking regions of the country, mass communication in English only, mixed marriages, and interaction with Anglo-Canadians at work, at church, and within the neighborhood (Tremblay 1961:232-241). Differential exposure to these influences results in different degrees of acculturation.

Another researcher has also been interested in accounting for differential rates of assimilation of French-speaking minority groups in Canada. Frank Vallee's approach involves studying a combination of variables (demographic-ecological, attitudinal-cultural, and social structural) to explain varying degrees of persistence in different regions, with persistence largely being measured in terms of French language use and retention by those claiming French origins (Vallee 1969; 1971). The key variable is a social structural feature, "community closure" or "institutional completeness." Institutional completeness refers to the existence of a full range of regional or community francophone institutions, such as economic and mutual benefit groups, educational, patriotic, and religious associations and organizations. Institutional completeness allows group autonomy and contributes to the creation of social power for the group in question. In terms of language retention, francophones in northeastern New Brunswick are identified by Vallee as being the least assimilated of all French-speaking minority groups in Canada, outside of those living in Quebec.

Vallee's attempt to formulate a comprehensive framework for generating and testing hypotheses is constructive, and comparative studies in French Canada are sorely needed. However, I consider the concept of community closure to have limitations as a key variable in accounting for persistence of Acadians in northeastern New Brunswick; its application there has several drawbacks.

First, institutional completeness of francophones in New Brunswick would seem to suggest the existence of a structurally plural society in the province. However, as I see it, this is the crux of one of the key differences between the structural position of Acadians in New Brunswick and that of Quebeckers in Canada. The ethnic group composition of the population in New Brunswick is parallel to that of the ethnic group composition of Canada as a whole; in New Brunswick, francophones represent about one-third of the population; in Canada, Quebeckers represent about one-quarter of the population. However, the manner in which the minority language groups are incorporated into each of the two territories in question is quite different. Quebeckers are members of an essentially francophone province possessing a full range of institutions to serve the francophone population; Quebec is a geographically and socio-culturally distinct territory incorporated at the federal level into a structurally plural nation. Quebeckers are incorporated into the federation as members of a group based in a distinct section of the nation. On the other hand, Acadians in New Brunswick are members of a cultural category in a culturally plural province; they are incorporated into the province as individuals.

There is no territory in New Brunswick strictly Acadian or francophone; there is no territory where most of the francophones of the province or only francophones live. Acadian leaders have recognized this as being something of a strategic problem. As a solution, it has been suggested that francophones in the southern part of the province could be dismissed and voluntarily lost to assimilation so that energies could be put into the strengthening of the Acadian position in the north (Poulin 1972).[5] Interestingly enough, this is something of the same strategy suggested by Quebec nationalists who dismiss Acadians in general as a cause perdue, a French-speaking minority already lost to acculturation. Public or provincial institutions cannot be considered francophone; at best they provide services for both language groups. This is precisely the issue regarding the provincial education system in New Brunswick today. Francophones have requested the creation of two sub-departments of education in New Brunswick, one to handle educational programs and policy for francophones and one for anglophones, but such a structural division has not yet taken place.[6]

Various private and exclusively francophone institutions of the type indicated by Vallee do exist in New Brunswick, e.g.,

Société de la Mutual Assomption (an insurance and financial institution), Société des Acadiens du Nouveau-Brunswick (a patriotic association and lobbying group), Parti Acadien (a political party), the Chambre de Commerce, and Club Richelieu (the last two being service or civic groups) among others. However, these institutions have varying degrees of influence within regions and communities, and within classes and age groupings of the francophone population as well. Although such organizations exist in the province, it remains to be ascertained just how much relevance the organizations have for residents and communities of northeastern New Brunswick or any other area of New Brunswick. For example, Parti Acadien appears to appeal largely to young adults, especially among those more educated than many of their fellows.[7] Club Richelieu, Société de la Mutual Assomption, Société des Acadiens du Nouveau-Brunswick, and the Chambre de Commerce have traditionally been relevant for professional people and businessmen among the francophone population. It is well-known that francophone institutions of prestige and influence are centered in Moncton; the importance of Société de la Mutual Assomption is considerable, one indication being the organization's recent financing of the construction of a large business complex in downtown Moncton. Recent calls for new leadership among francophones in New Brunswick have been triggered by the feeling that institutions such as Société de la Mutual Assomption and Société des Acadiens du Nouveau-Brunswick have lost touch with the needs and interests of the francophone populace in the province as a whole.[8]

Vallee has indicated the need to ascertain the degree of individual participation in these francophone institutions and, thus, the importance of these institutions in different regions and in different segments of the francophone population (Vallee 1969). Here I simply underline that the existence of such institutions within the province or within one region of the province does not indicate that they are particularly relevant for most residents of most areas of the province.

In addition, Vallee's use of community closure or group autonomy as a key variable to explain group persistence lends little to the study of inter-ethnic relations per se, and, in fact, it would seem to blur the picture of the society in question by omitting consideration of Anglo-Canadians in northern and eastern New Brunswick. About 37 percent of the population in northern and eastern New Brunswick (counties of Gloucester, Kent, Madawaska, Northumberland, Restigouche, Victoria, and Westmoreland) are of English origin. Are we to understand that the two ethnic groups in the area are isolated from each other? Are we to assume that community closure also includes community isolation and self-sufficiency? Are there no contacts between anglophones and francophones as groups and individuals? In essence, such an approach precludes the study of ongoing relations between the two ethnic groups.

OBJECTIVES OF THIS STUDY

Frederik Barth has suggested that by understanding the nature of relations and contacts between ethnic groups one is able to approach understanding the persistence of groups. Barth wrote;

> ethnic distinctions do not depend on an absence of social interaction and acceptance, but are quite the contrary often the very foundations on which embracing social systems are built. Interaction in such a social system does not lead to its liquidation through change and acculturation; cultural differences can persist despite inter-ethnic contact and interdependence (Barth 1969a:10).

In this vein, I consider that the persistence or acculturation of Acadians in New Brunswick can profitably be studied through an examination of the structure of contacts which exist between Acadians and Anglo-Canadians in the province. By structure of contacts, I specifically mean the relatively permanent and patterned ways in which the members of the two ethnic groups engage in face-to-face interaction.

Examining the structure of contacts between Acadians and Anglo-Canadians has particular relevance in attempting to understand group persistence precisely because of the traditional measure of that persistence: language use and retention. The use of this measure has been criticized as being less than complete (Vallee 1969:90) and the census categories on which the measure is based are criticized as being imprecise (Joy 1972:137-38), but the measure is practical and in general use by most authors concerned with the topic; thus I will use language retention as an indicator of ethnic persistence. If one accepts the assumption that retention and use of the French language by those claiming French origins indicate that these individuals have persisted in being Acadian, the question then becomes why does someone of French language and origin adopt English to the exclusion of his own mother tongue? Why does an Acadian learn English and why does he stop using French?

Most usually an Acadian learns English because he wishes, needs, or is forced, to communicate to an English speaker, probably an Anglo-Canadian. Most Anglo-Canadians do not become bilingual. Undoubtedly this is a reflection of the fact that, in many social situations (e.g., in work), Anglo-Canadians have had the superordinate position, and it was incumbent upon the subordinate francophone to learn English. If verbal communication is to transpire between Acadian and Anglo-Canadian, then it is the Acadian who becomes bilingual. Some Acadians in northeastern New Brunswick are bilingual, especially those living in urban areas such as Bathurst. Many others living in rural areas remain French monolingual. To understand why this is so, an appropriate field of research is the examination of the structure of contacts existing between such Acadians and Anglo-Canadians in the area.

Denton has argued convincingly that assimilation of French Canadians was negligible after the fall of Canada not because of an absence of contacts between the French and the British colonists, but because particular residential, political, and economic patterns discouraged the creation of contacts that would integrate the two ethnic groups (1966). Similarly, the sociocultural patterns structuring contacts between Acadians and Anglo-Canadians help account for the limited learning of English by rural dwelling Acadians and the limited English language adoption by such people. The contacts between members of the two ethnic groups are channelled and minimized in such a way as to limit the necessity of many Acadians to learn English.

The following chapters will examine the structure of contacts between residents of one rural Acadian village and Anglo-Canadians with a view to understanding how contacts are channelled so that, in Barth's terms, exclusion of Anglo-Canadians is maintained and incorporation of local Acadians encouraged.

THE REGION

French-English relations in Canada are colored by longstanding concerns regarding language use and the survival of the French-speaking minority. However, those general concerns take on various particular forms reflecting provincial and regional differences. In Maritime Canada, Acadians are found in a range of circumstances affecting their language use and their survival as French-speaking people. One such context is that of northeastern New Brunswick (see Map 1), wherein Ste. Marie-sur-Mer is located.

STE. MARIE-SUR-MER

In many ways Ste. Marie-sur-Mer is representative of northeastern New Brunswick. Although Ste. Marie is not presented here as a "type" village, it is nonetheless similar to many area villages in terms of the ethnic, demographic, and economic features of its residents. Like most other inhabitants of Lameque Island and Gloucester County, the 387 villagers of Ste. Marie are French-speaking, Catholic, and largely descendants of Acadians.

Northeastern New Brunswick is largely rural; the region contains few settlements composed of one thousand people or more. The largest community on Lameque Island, also called Lameque, has a population of 935; another 5,200 of the island's residents are

THE REGION   39

distributed in the seventeen named settlements around its coasts
(Statistics Canada 1973).

Northeastern New Brunswick (i.e., Gloucester County, Restigouche
County, and Alnick Parish in Northumberland County) is characterized
by high outmigration of working age adults, high birth rates, and,
concomittantly, a population in which a great number are economically non-productive young people (Even 1970:76-109 passim); 44
percent of the population is less than fifteen years of age and 60
percent is less than twenty-five years of age (Even 1970:77-79).
In Ste. Marie 40 percent of the population is less than fifteen years
of age, 62 percent is less than twenty-five, and 5 percent is sixty-
five years or more; hence, the proportion of active adults in Ste.
Marie is similar to that for the area as a whole.

Rural villagers of northeastern New Brunswick have traditionally
engaged in primary industries, either fishing, farming, or lumbering;
residents of Ste. Marie rely on the fishery as the major source of
their income. The region is economically depressed; about three-
fourths of the gainfully employed villagers of Ste. Marie are
seasonally unemployed.

In general Ste. Marie reflects many characteristics of the wider
region of which it is a part, and it is appropriate to provide a
fuller description of that region.

PHYSICAL GEOGRAPHY

Northeastern New Brunswick is located in the Eastern Lowlands
of the Maritime Basin, the latter which includes all of the southwestern part of the Gulf of St. Lawrence, the eastern half of New
Brunswick, all of Prince Edward Island, and sections of Nova Scotia.

Putnam has described these lowlands as "flat and swampy, with the drainage having been deranged by glaciation. Much of the plain is covered with deep sandy drift, but in places the rock lies almost at the surface over broad areas" (1952:74-75). The rock is of sandstone, shale, and limestone; these geological deposits in conjunction with a climate featuring "long, cold winters; short cool summers; and a natural forest vegetation composed largely of coniferous trees such as pine, spruce, and balsam fir" all contribute to northeastern New Brunswick's characteristic "acidic, leached, and infertile" soil (Putnam 1952:84).

For the most part, the eastern coastal lowlands of New Brunswick do not share in the extensive commercial forests which are one of the province's most valuable resources. In the poorly drained, sandy or boggy soils of the eastern coastal areas, woodlands are not extensive and are limited to growths of black spruce, cedar, tamarack, white and wire birches, and jack pines; red spruce, yellow birch, beech, and sugar maple are found in some of the better locations (Putnam 1952:83).

Though Nova Scotia possesses considerable deposits of coal, gold, salt, and gypsum and potentially valuable offshore oil deposits, New Brunswick's economically important mineral resources are presently known to be located near Bathurst and are limited to deposits of base metals, particularly zinc and lead (Baudry 1966:35).

The resources of longstanding importance to residents of New Brunswick's eastern coastal lowlands have been those of the sea. The offshore fishing resources include "200,000 square miles of shallow sea comprising the greatest fishing grounds on the earth" (Putnam 1952:99). The richest of these offshore fishing grounds are king. Some 1,000 Acadians escaped immediate deportation by fleeing their homes in the Nova Scotian farmlands and seeking refuge in French-held areas elsewhere--in today's Cape Breton, Prince Edward Island, Quebec, and New Brunswick. However, by 1760, the year of the fall of the rest of New France to Britain, many of those Acadians hiding in various settlements in the area had been rounded up and deported by the British (LeBlanc:1970).

Provisions of the 1763 Treaty of Paris allowed the return of Acadians to Maritime Canada, and by 1771 there were about 1,500 Acadians in New Brunswick, many of whom were located in the St. John River Valley of southwestern New Brunswick. The late eighteenth century also brought an influx of English, Scotch, Irish, and Loyalist settlers, from the New England colonies, into Maritime Canada. Acadians were directly or indirectly compelled to leave the southwestern area of New Brunswick, and they removed themselves to locations along the Bay of Chaleur, the eastern coast of New Brunswick, and along the valleys of the Memramcook and Madawaska Rivers (Arsenault 1966:232-33). In northern New Brunswick, these Acadians were joined by other countrymen who were returning from points of exile in France and elsewhere, as well as by Norman-French settlers from Quebec. In 1804, a church census reported that 900 Acadians inhabited the northern counties of Gloucester and Restigouche alone, and that nearly 3,800 Acadians were located in New Brunswick (Arsenault 1966:240); the latter figure represents a doubling of the province's French population in only thirty years.

The patterns of settlement and population distribution of French and English in New Brunswick were established during the nineteenth century and these patterns have persisted to the present. Irish, Scotch, and English settlers entered the northern and eastern sections of New Brunswick in the nineteenth century, but, except for what were to become urban areas such as Bathurst, the Anglo-Canadian and Acadian settlements have remained relatively separated from one another.

In rural areas, especially in northern and eastern New Brunswick, there are villages, or stretches of settlement along the roads, that are French (or English) and which contain few, if any, of the opposite ethnic group. For example, the shore road along the Bay of Chaleur is characterized by a clear and locally recognized break between French-speaking populations and their properties in lower Gloucester County and those of the predominantly English-speaking settlements from New Bandon to Bathurst. Generally northeastern New Brunswick rural settlements founded as French (or as English) in the nineteenth century have remained as French (or English) until today.

For over a century, from their return after the grand dérangement until the end of the nineteenth century, many Acadians remained relatively isolated from each other, from Quebeckers, and from Anglo-Canadians. Acadians initially settled areas which had been largely rejected by English-speaking settlers; these areas were less attractive than those elsewhere in the province because of their isolation, harshness of climate, and poor soil quality. Sometimes living in areas that were only accessible by water, the Acadians grew in numbers and, it has been suggested, survived because of their seclusion (see, for example, Baudry 1966, especially his Chapter Ten). Just as Acadians ignored the outside world which they had learned to mistrust, so too did the outside world ignore them.

THE REGION 45

The few schools, colleges, and hospitals which were located in Acadian areas were usually run by religious orders of the Catholic Church; Acadian contacts with government authorities and agencies were apparently minimal through much of the nineteenth century (Thorburn 1961:23).

The twentieth century, however, has witnessed ever increasing contacts between Acadians and Anglo-Canadians. The reasons for this increased contact result from historical events and socio-economic changes in the area and North America as a whole. For example, two world wars brought Acadians and Anglo-Canadians together in performing military duty. Some Acadians who returned from overseas military duty brought war brides, a few of whom were English.

In the second and third decades of this century, Acadians went to New England in search of wage labor. In later decades, Acadians migrated to Detroit, Michigan, and Windsor, Ontario, in search of work. Today some of these Acadians have reestablished homes in the Maritimes, while others periodically visit the Maritimes and make their permanent homes elsewhere. Acadians who return home after having spent years abroad bring with them knowledge of the English language and English Canadian and American customs.

Although Acadians were able to maintain their ethnic identity by applying tenacity and sacrifice in the face of hardship, fears have increased that they may not be able to retain their identity in the face of increasing contacts with English-speakers and involvement in an urban Anglo-dominated milieu. For many Acadians adoption of English language and customs has been a means to facilitate ac-

ceptance and success in urban areas. Name changes, e.g., from
"LeBlanc" to "White," plus a change in religion and adoption of the
English language have been tactics purposefully employed by some
who wanted entry into that sector of Canadian society controlled by
Anglo-Canadians. It is impossible to know, however, how many
individuals and whole families have been voluntarily acculturated
by these means.

REGIONAL SOCIAL FEATURES

Economy and Social Welfare

The most important source of employment for francophones in New
Brunswick has been in primary industries--agriculture, fishing, and
forestry (Raîche 1962:97; Baudry 1966:49). In the Shippegan area,
however, agriculture and forestry are of limited importance. A
recent government survey described the soil in the area as
"physically marginal for sustained arable agriculture"; it was also
noted that "at best, forestry in the Shippegan area may be considered
as a source of supplemental income for woodlot owners" (Community
Improvement Corporation Planning Department 1968). The fishery is
the most important primary industry employing local men; about 40
percent of the rural labor force in the civil parish are fishermen.

Although there are large-scale wood pulp processing plants and
mining and smelting operations in the Bathurst region, in the
Shippegan area secondary industry is confined to a half dozen major
fish processing plants (usines) and several peat moss plants. Fishing and fish processing employ about 60 percent of the rural labor
force in the parish. About 90 percent of the usine workers are

women; this type of work is practically the only source of employment available for area women (Community Improvement Corporation Planning Department 1968).

In earlier years the peat moss plants provided employment for large numbers of local people, but recent mechanization in the collection and drying of the moss has greatly reduced the need for workers. In spite of the opening of new plants on Lameque Island, less than two hundred area people are employed in this industry today.

Both the _usines_ and the peat moss plants only operate during the warm months, approximately May through November. Fishing in the Shippegan area is limited to the same months, when the waters are free of ice. Nearly 80 percent of the rural labor force in the Shippegan area is unemployed from December through April (Community Improvement Corporation Planning Department 1968); residents rely on unemployment insurance payments to see them through this period. Social assistance is needed by many families for whom unemployment payments do not provide sufficient income. Residents of the area, like all Canadians, are entitled to receive old age pensions, veterans' pensions, disability pensions, child and youth allowances; since 1970, medical and hospital care are almost totally free.

Employment in the region is highly seasonal and yields low financial returns. Average incomes in New Brunswick and Gloucester County are low. In 1971 the average annual salary for a man in New Brunswick was $5,042 and that for a woman $2,282; in rural non-farm Gloucester County, a man's average annual salary was $3,509 and a woman's $1,769. The average family income in Shippegan Parish was only 51 percent of the average for Canada as a whole ($4,913: $9,600) (Statistics Canada 1973).

Combined with northeastern New Brunswick's poverty have been serious problems in health and education. Specifically, in 1961, 26 percent of the adult population in Shippegan Civil Parish was illiterate; another 44 percent had finished four years of schooling; 28 percent more had completed eight years of schooling, and about 1 percent of the population had attended high school. (Société d'Aménagement Regional Service d'Urbanisme 1968:26-27). In 1971 the population in Gloucester County could still be characterized as under-educated. Fourteen percent of adults had attained less than grade four, and 45 percent had attained less than grade nine (Statistics Canada 1973).[1]

A 1951 health survey revealed that New Brunswick was the Canadian province having the second highest frequencies of infant mortality, maternity death, and tuberculosis. The French counties (i.e., those counties having two-thirds or more francophone population) were considered as the areas which had contributed greatly to the province's overall poor record (Baudry 1966:15).

The complex of socioeconomic problems chronic to northeastern New Brunswick has become the rationale for extensive governmental programs of change there. Several hundred million dollars of federal funds have been approved for use in the area since the mid-1960s. Relatively immediate changes have been effected through school construction, consolidation of school districts, and the closing of one-room school houses. Long range goals involve improvements in various aspects of life, including the rationalization of the inshore fishery.

THE REGION   49

Communication and Transportation

A French-language daily newspaper and radio-television broadcasting are available to residents of northeastern New Brunswick. However, the newspaper, l'Évangéline, is published in Moncton, and television broadcasting is from Quebec, as is some of the radio broadcasting. Two weekly French-language newspapers published in northeastern New Brunswick provide local news, and l'Évangéline includes coverage of area news as well. Nonetheless, in comparison to areas elsewhere in the province, the francophones here have relatively little locally produced media coverage.

Transportation facilities are similarly limited. Bus and passenger train connections to major points must be made in Bathurst; plane connections are normally made in Moncton, 150 miles from Lameque. A limited number of daily flights are also available at two small regional airports, each located about 75 miles from Lameque. Connecting settlements along the North Shore is a private bus line which makes leisurely runs each day between Shippegan and Bathurst and between Shippegan and Tracadie.

Highways leading to northeastern New Brunswick are few. The Trans-Canadian Highway (#2), the main highway carrying east and west traffic between Nova Scotia and Quebec, cuts across the southern and western parts of New Brunswick (see Map 2). Highways which lead to, or traverse, northeastern New Brunswick are of varying quality. The annual spring thaw churns up pavement and creates cracks and potholes of sometimes considerable proportions in the roads. It is not unusual for portions of Highway 8, which forms part of the inland road between Moncton and Bathurst, and Highway 11, between Moncton and the Tracadie-Shippegan-Caraquet area, to be functionally "one lane" in the early spring. Depending on the season, and the particular road, the regional highways are passable to moderately good.

People in the Shippegan area have only enjoyed conveniences such as paved roads, electricity, and telephones for the last twenty years or so. In addition, prior to 1959, Lameque Island residents travelled to the mainland via a ferry, when the water was open, and crossed the ice in winter by foot or by vehicle. For several weeks each year crossings could not be made; there was too much ice to allow the use of the ferry, but the ice was too thin to allow passage over it. In 1959 a bridge was opened which now allows travel from island to mainland all year round. Miscou residents must still rely on a small open-deck scow propelled by boat, to cross the waters to Lameque Island in the warm months; they cross by any means available in the winter. There still remain several weeks each year when Miscou residents are unable to cross the waters and are cut off from Lameque Island and the mainland.

Service Centers and Facilities

Lameque Island can be thought of as a point in several circles representing governmental and ecclesiastical domains. The greater the distance between the island and the administrative centers of these domains, the lesser is the daily influence and importance of the domains for island residents.

Bathurst (population c. 16,000) is the county seat of Gloucester County and the location of the Catholic Church's diocesan headquarters in northeastern New Brunswick. The city provides the largest shopping facilities in the area, has a large new hospital and a four-year French-language college. Thus, various governmental, educational, religious, and health services emanate from Bathurst. Nevertheless, most people in the Shippegan area rarely go to Bathurst; such trips are usually made only in emergency or unusual situations, e.g. to pick up someone from the train, to visit someone in the hospital. Exceptions are local students who attend the college in Bathurst on a full-time or part-time basis.

Various government offices are located within the civil parish itself. Shippegan town contains a Royal Canadian Mounted Police (RCMP) detachment, a New Brunswick Department of Youth and Welfare Office, and a Federal Department of Fisheries office. Most people in the Shippegan area shop for household goods, clothing, furniture and the like in Shippegan town or Lameque (Community Improvement Corporation Planning Department 1968) or order merchandise through mail order catalogues from Eatons and Simpson-Sears, both large department store chains. Grocery stores are located in Lameque, Shippegan town, and at various places within the civil parish where population clusters are of sufficient size to support such stores.

A small hospital capable of handling emergencies and simple health problems is located in Lameque. Patients with serious injuries or illnesses are sent to larger hospitals in urban centers such as Bathurst, St. John, Moncton, Campbellton, or Edmundston. There are two medical doctors in the Shippegan area, but no dentists or optometrists. Because of the general lack of locally based trained medical practitioners, appointments with dentists and optometrists must be made several months in advance. Large distances must be covered to reach the practitioners that do exist in the area. A trip to the optometrist's office in Caraquet (or to the dentist's office in Tracadie) requires a journey of fifty or sixty miles for someone from Lameque Island.

The island contains several local elementary schools (grades one through six). The student population for each school comes from an area that normally corresponds to a village or an ecclesiastical parish. Students attend grades seven, eight, and nine at the recently completed junior high school in Lameque town. A high school and trade school are located on the mainland in Shippegan town.

A small collège classique in Shippegan town has offered local girls four years of training which lead to Bachelor of Arts or Bachelor of Education degrees. In the future, however, only two-year programs will be offered. Students from the area also attend Collège de Bathurst and Université de Moncton. Occasionally, area students have won scholarships allowing them to pursue post-secondary training in French-language universities elsewhere in Canada or France.

The Roman Catholic Church on Lameque Island has ecclesiastical parishes centered at Lameque town, St. Raphael-sur-Mer, and Petite Riviére de l'Île; a mission church is located in the village of Pigeon Hill and is served by the priest from St. Raphael. There are no parochial schools on the island, but some nuns teach secular classes in the public schools. No Protestant churches have resident ministers on a year-long basis; occasionally young ministers are assigned the area as a summer mission.

Entertainment facilities are not abundant in the Shippegan area. The movie house in Shippegan town burned down several years ago and was never rebuilt. A drive-in movie theatre was recently opened on the island and operates during the warm months of the year. Several summer fishing festivals and winter carnivals are presented annually; Sunday bingo and Saturday night dances are regular occurrences all year long. Occasionally a spectacle, a night of vocal and instrumental music, is presented under the sponsorship of local schools, French-language colleges or universities, and government agencies. Like all Canadians, be they francophone or anglophone, hockey consumes a greal deal of leisure time from November to May. My hometown, St. Louis, Missouri, was immediately familiar to local people as being the home of les Blues of the National Hockey League.

Thus, as described in this chapter, after their return from the grand dérangement in the eighteenth century, Acadians established their settlements in some of the poorer areas of New Brunswick, those areas of less interest to English-speaking settlers. Since that time Acadians of northeastern New Brunswick have continued to pay a high price for their relative isolation; in standards of health, education, and income, these Acadians have achieved less than individuals living in more prosperous areas of the province.

Since the survival of Acadians as an ethnic and linguistic group has been explained or accounted for by their poverty and isolation, it would seem to follow that prosperity and entrance into provincial and national life would endanger Acadian survival and hasten the group's acculturation. This conclusion may not be warranted, however, if other cultural factors figure in the maintenance of Acadian identity in settings such as Ste. Marie. Before turning to an examination of cultural influences on inter-ethnic contacts of villagers, I next describe the nature of the village itself.

THE VILLAGE

This chapter describes basic features of Ste. Marie, many of which will be dealt with in more detail in subsequent chapters. This overview of village life is presented in order to facilitate the reader's understanding of individual chapters below.

SETTLEMENT PATTERN

A visitor to Ste. Marie gets the best visual perspective of the village from the sea, thus viewing the land as the fishermen do. Fishermen returning from the inshore grounds first catch sight of the land when the steeple of the St. Raphael Parish church appears on the horizon; with this marker, men see their way home. As the boats gradually pull closer to land, the distribution of the eastern coastal communities on Lameque Island becomes more distinct. To the south is the village of Chiasson Office, physically isolated from the other eastern coastal communities by Grand Lac and an extensive peat bog, and socially separated from these communities by its position in a different ecclesiastical parish. Chiasson Office, like many other place-names, reflects the importance of a non-physical English presence in a region inhabited almost totally by French-speakers. The English names are pronounced with an Acadian accent and the origin of the names has been forgotten or ignored by local francophones.

To the north of Chiasson Office, and on the other side of the peat bog, lies the village of Ste. Marie-sur-Mer, location of the wharf used by inshore fishermen of St. Raphael Parish. Above Ste. Marie is the village of St. Raphael-sur-Mer, the approximate north-south center of the ecclesiastical parish, which contains the church, elementary school, community center, and cooperative grocery store used by residents of Ste. Marie.

As seen from the sea, the settlement pattern in Ste. Marie clearly reflects the three neighborhoods in the village; between the string of houses lying along the coastal road are two areas of open unused ground which serve to demarcate the three neighborhoods (see Map 3). Also discernible is the character of early land holdings by which individual properties ran in long parallel strips from the shore across the cleared, inhabited, and tilled land, into the interior woodlands. Today many of these strips are broken into blocks as house lots, but the original pattern remains visible. Differences in house construction styles indicate the pattern of physical growth in the number of village houses and reflect, too, the division of individual parcels of land through time.

No matter the age or construction of village houses, nearly all are painted in bright colors with window and door frames in shades contrasting with those of exterior walls and roof; against the banks of winter snow these shades take on added brilliance, lending color to an otherwise almost totally white and grey world. Finally, from the sea, one can see several small boats beached along the shore and the traps or nets or other assorted fishing gear which clearly indicate that here live a seagoing people, a village of fishermen.

NEIGHBORHOOD AND HOUSEHOLD

The village is about two-and-one-half miles long, and three neighborhoods can be delineated within it. Paulin Road is one-half mile long and is the most southerly neighborhood. The name "Paulin Road" is recent to the neighborhood. A few years ago a provincial highway department crew erected the sign identifying that portion of the village as Paulin Road, but supposedly the name had never been previously used by villagers. The sign has remained, although some villagers are puzzled regarding its origins, and occasionally today the name Paulin Road is used. More commonly, this end of the village is simply called "Ste. Marie," as is the central section of the village.

Paulin Road contains two small épiceries, shops where food-stuffs, such as dairy products, bread, and canned goods, are sold. One of the épiceries doubles as a recreation center and provides a jukebox and pinball machines. An automobile repair shop, sawmill (both rarely open), and several rental chalets are also located on Paulin Road. There are thirty households on Paulin Road.

The middle section of Ste. Marie contains the largest grocery store in the village, several chalets for rent, a recreation center featuring jukebox and billiard tables, the wharf used by inshore fishermen, a usine which pickles herring, and a small shop which salts and dries cod; there are twenty-nine households in this section of Ste. Marie.

L'autre bout de la plaine (or l'autre bout) is three-tenths of a mile long and is the most northerly section of the village, located on the far side of an open plain. About fifty yards of uncleared land lie between this section and the next cluster of houses to the north. The northern boundary of Ste. Marie is not uniformly recognized by villagers; some suggest that the village extends for another half-mile in the direction of the parish church; other villagers recognize a less extensive area as being Ste. Marie. In addition, voting districts and postal services delineate slightly different boundaries for the village.

In l'autre bout are located one rental chalet and one food-stand offering sandwiches, soda, and ice cream to summer tourists and passersby; there are twelve households in this neighborhood. The cooperative grocery store in the village of St. Raphael is about a half-mile from this section of the village and is closer for residents of l'autre bout than is the store in Ste. Marie; hence, residents of this section of the village commonly shop in St. Raphael rather than in Ste. Marie.

Approximately half of the village households do not include members who own a truck or car and, thus, daily shopping must be done on foot or by bicycle; such shopping is virtually confined to the neighborhood in which one resides. Individuals with cars are likely to stop by the village's largest grocery store at least once or twice a week; in addition, they frequently stop at their neighborhood épicerie and at the cooperative stores in St. Raphael and Lameque.

The frequent shopping at several stores allows the maintenance of good relations with village storekeepers who permit credit arrangements to be made. Stores provide a meeting place or a clearing house for news and exchanging of information. The time spent in such stores varies according to the age, sex, and individual involved. A few men may daily spend up to an hour in the village's largest grocery store. Women and children seldom pass time in the stores.

Each neighborhood provides its residents similar services in the stores and recreation centers; residents of l'autre bout receive such services in the village of St. Raphael. Similarly, natural resources of neighborhoods are largely the same and utilized by the residents of each neighborhood. Children play within their own neighborhood; families make use of their neighborhood beach for recreational boating and fishing; berry picking is done by individuals within the wooded areas of their own neighborhood. Thus each neighborhood is an important base of social interaction, especially for village women and children.

A one or two story house and a few storage or work sheds are usually associated with each household. Most barns have been torn down; green cellars have fallen into disuse and disappeared; very few people have garages to house automobiles or trucks. A garden, an area in which wood is cut and stacked, and perhaps a small enclosure for domestic fowl are additional work areas associated with some households.

Outdoor areas have traditionally been for work, not for adult recreation. Today it is only on very warm days or evenings that villagers will be found sitting outside on porches. Many homes do not even have porches. It is common for houses to have a front door to which neither steps nor porch is built; the door is essentially useless except in emergencies. Back doors or side doors rarely have a porch on which more than one person can sit. With the exception of sports events, social or recreational activity generally takes place indoors.

The kitchen is the center of daylong household activity: the day's activity begins there as early as three or three-thirty on summer mornings when inshore fishermen have their breakfasts; the day's activity ends there when householders have their "lunch" (tea or coffee and perhaps a light snack) before retiring. Much of the woman's work is done in the kitchen where she prepares meals, does laundry, and sews. Clothes washing machines, sewing machines, and large appliances are generally located in the kitchen or in a small adjoining utility room. Children do homework on the large kitchen table; the kitchen table is used for card playing by householders of all ages. Visitors are received in the kitchen unless the occasion is particularly formal, at which time the guests may be admitted to a living room, if one exists. The television is usually installed close to the kitchen where it is conveniently heard, if not seen, by all householders.

ECONOMIC, SOCIAL, AND RECREATIONAL ACTIVITIES

As three-fourths of the jobs held by villagers are related to the fishery, a preoccupation with fishing colors much of village life. For example, within houses are various souvenirs of the sea --arrangements of odd shells and rocks, mounted hulks of huge lobsters, unusually shaped driftwood varnished and attached to stands, and miniature lobster traps made of popsicle sticks. Such items are often fashioned to sell to passing tourists or to give to friends and relatives, but just as often they are made simply to decorate the home. The ocean is an endless source of interest, pleasure, and tragedy, as well as the major source of income for villagers. The activities of village fishermen in the inshore and offshore fisheries will be discussed in some detail in Chapter Five.

Activities within the fishery are determined by the seasons. The cold months preclude gainful employment for most villagers and the seasons similarly guide other activities such as the production and preparation of foodstuffs for household consumption. In mid-May villagers spend several long days preparing the soil and planting vegetable gardens. Throughout the summer the gardens are given varying degrees of attention, according to the gardener's interest. By the first of September there is danger of frost and by late September the garden produce has been gathered and preserving of it has begun.

During the fall, domestic fowl are killed, fish are salted and dried for home consumption, ducks and geese are hunted. Villagers lucky enough to win a license in the annual license draw hunt moose.

Many households have large deep-freezers and great quantities of vegetables, berries, fish, fowl, and meat fill the freezers by the end of fall. In addition, lobster and crab are canned, clams, vegetables, jams, and jellies are bottled, and a few individuals make wine.

Any outside repairs or construction must be done in the warm months. Outer shells of houses are constructed in the summer and fall; inner finishing is done in the winter. During the winter fishermen repair and build fishing equipment, particularly lobster traps, nets, and trawl lines. The repairing and painting of boats in late April signal the end of the "dead" season and the approach of another "busy" season.

Social and recreational activities are also guided by the seasons. Sports activities of young men and boys vary with the season; hockey is the winter favorite, softball that of summer. However, for most people in the village summer is the busy work season. The hours are long and the work hard. Fishermen and *usine* workers have little time or energy left to expend as participants or observers at the sports field.

Winter has the reputation of being the "fun" part of the year. Nightly card games in individual homes or weekly games at the parish community center are popular pastimes, and a few villagers have snowmobiles which are used for recreation. Finally, in February or March, just prior to the beginning of Lent, a Winter Carnival is held by St. Raphael Parish; the affair is mainly enjoyed by young people and children who take part in sport competitions, costuming contests, and dances.

The Canadian winter undoubtedly influences social interaction in various areas of the country. In a study made in a section of Toronto, interpersonal contacts were found to vary according to the season and its weather; winter social life was characterized by increased interaction between neighbors and friends living in close proximity; during the summer these Torontonians more commonly visited friends and relatives beyond the local neighborhood (Michelson 1971). In a similar fashion, activity in Ste. Marie is locally restricted during the winter; contacts with kin and relatives residing beyond the immediate area are commonly enjoyed in the summer months when relatives from various areas return to the village to spend vacations away from summer heat and urbanization. Residents of Ste. Marie are too busy earning their annual income to be able to visit elsewhere in the summer months. Nonetheless, the climate and location of the village, as well as the attraction of "going home," make the summer a busy season for visiting and reunions with kin and friends.

Social activities in the village are also affected by the liturgical calendar of the Catholic Church. The setting of wedding dates provides an example of how social activity is influenced by both the season and the liturgical calendar. Nearly eighty percent of all parish weddings in the last twenty-five years took place in the last six months of the calendar year. The season of Lent takes place during about two months of the first half of the year, and during this time marriages are not normally performed by the Church. Also during the first six months of the year, incomes are low and villagers are preparing for, or have just begun, the work season. Villagers are busy and short of cash needed for wedding expenses. Marriages are not usually performed during Advent, the four weeks before Christmas; however, just prior to, and immediately after, Advent are favorite times for marriages. November, when all the fishing and related work at _usines_ has been completed, is the most frequently chosen month in which weddings are performed.

As a season of fasting and abstinence, Lent has changed radically; today the practicing of denial during Lent is largely up to the choice and discretion of the individual. Saturday night soirées for parish adults are cancelled during Lent, but this involves, at most, one or two such affairs. Christmas and Easter remain important church holy days and holidays when kinsmen are visited.

Villagers also engage in year-round social and recreational activities. People with access to automobiles and with extra money may go to the drive-in cinema, to weekly bingo games in Lameque, or to dances held in the area. A villager may spend only two or three dollars at a bingo game and perhaps win that much in return. However, expenses in entrance fees and drinks for a couple at a dance may be ten dollars or more and, thus, the cost is prohibitive for many villagers.

Youngsters may go to the village recreation hall to play billiards and listen to music or to one store to play the pinball machines and jukebox. There is, however, no one spot in the village where adults congregate. At least one of the three stores will be visited daily by a representative of most households; men, more often than women, are likely to stop at the stores. Through their frequent use of telephones women can keep up on village news and gossip without leaving their homes.

Weekly attendance at Mass provides an opportunity to see and greet villagers or parishioners, but conversations at Mass are brief and usually transpire between men prior to their entering the church.

For most villagers visiting is casual and informal. During the week individuals may drop by a house for a few minutes or may pay more extended visits of an hour or so; over the weekends many villagers visit each other in Ste. Marie or in the parish or

THE VILLAGE 65

wider area.

During the year, births, marriages, and deaths infrequently bring relatives and/or villagers together on a more formal basis. Invitations are extended for special aspects of each event such as the baptism itself, the private family prayers prior to the church funeral, or the wedding dinner. Special statuses, such as godparents, pallbearers, and master of ceremonies at the wedding dinner, are recognized in these situations; gifts are exchanged and acknowledged, e.g., presents for the new baby, Masses said for the deceased, the loan of a new car to the newly-married couple for their wedding day festivities.

In general then, village life is basically ordinary and orderly. Season and climate govern economic activities, such as fishing and gardening, as well as recreational and social activities. The spring thaw and the winter freeze are as regular and reliable as the liturgical seasons of Lent and Advent, and all combine to provide a familiar context for the year's unfolding.

Filling in the seasons are unexceptional days of casual interaction, occasionally disrupted by births, marriages, and deaths. In these life crises, as interpreted through church ritual, individuals are provided with a structure for ordering their own lives and for appraising changes in the lives of others.

From these general chapters concerning Canada, northeastern New Brunswick, and Ste. Marie-sur-Mer, I now turn to a more detailed description of aspects of village life which particularly influence the persistence of villagers as Acadians.

MAKING A LIVING

This chapter describes economic activities of villagers, especially those activities associated with the fishery. Of particular interest are the ways in which economic activities systematically minimize the creation of contacts between villagers and Anglo-Canadians.

SOURCES OF INCOME

Thirty-eight of the village's seventy-seven gainfully employed males are fishermen (Table II). It is rare to find a man who has not fished for a living at some time in his life, and several men have spent over fifty years of their working lives in the fishery. All women in the village have had husbands or brothers, and fathers or sons, who were fishermen. About one-third of the jobs held by villagers are those held by women, and the majority of these jobs are in usines, or fish processing plants; an additional 17 percent of the employed village men hold jobs in usines. Thus, about three-fourths of all employed villagers are engaged in some aspect of the fishery, either in bringing in the catch or in processing it.

Five to six months each year, the Shippegan area shores and harbors are closed by ice. When fishing is halted and the usines closed, villagers turn to savings and unemployment insurance pay-

Table II

Occupations of Villagers, Ste. Marie-sur-Mer*

Seasonal Jobs		Men	Women
Fishery			
inshore fisherman		22	
offshore fisherman		16	
laborer in *usine*		13	20
	Subtotals	51	20
	Seasonal Job Totals		71
Non-seasonal Jobs			
construction worker		8	
bus or truck driver		3	
teacher		3	2
orderly		1	
woodsman		2	
salesclerk, waitress		1	3
office worker		2	1
office or store manager		2	
owner of business		4	5**
	Subtotals	26	11
	Non-seasonal Job Totals		37
TOTALS			108

*Listed here is each individual's primary job, the job which supplies the largest part of his/her income.

**Four of the five women listed as being owners of businesses are assisted by their husbands and might best be considered as partners with their husbands. Though the business may be in the woman's name, it would be inaccurate to assume that the woman does all the work or has the major responsibility in the venture.

ments to support themselves, and, when necessary, obtain welfare payments to supplement insufficient incomes.

ACTIVITY CYCLES

Economic activity follows several different cycles during the course of a year. Non-seasonal workers, such as hospital orderlies, clerks, and storekeepers, have a regular work schedule throughout the year. School teachers work ten months and have holidays in July and August.

Because of the number of villagers involved in the fishery and associated industries, the most important work cycle is that based in the contrasting "dead" and "busy" seasons. During the dead season, running from approximately November through March, fishermen rest and prepare their boats, traps, nets, lines, and general equipment for use during the busy season; <u>usine</u> workers catch up on household tasks left undone over the summer months.

The Inshore Fishery

The inshore and offshore fisheries are different kinds of occupations based on different cycles of activity. Some of the more significant differences between the two fisheries are discussed in the following pages.

The inshore fishery of Ste. Marie is a small-scale, labor intensive, daily enterprise. Crews seldom include more than three men. Most boats fish lobster and groundfish in waters off the eastern shore of Lameque Island; round trip distances covered daily usually do not exceed twenty miles.

If weather permits, fishing is carried out every day in season except Sunday when fishing for profit is prohibited by law. The lobster season is officially open from May 1 through June 30; groundfish are fished in July, August, and part of September, depending on the weather. If there are fall herring runs inshore, fishermen with larger boats will participate in this fishery for as long as the runs last, which is seldom more than a week or two at the end of August or first part of September.

There are two types of boats used in the inshore fishery. A bateau is an open boat, running between 30 and 35 feet in length; it is powered by a marine engine and guided by the use of a rear tiller. A pinque is equipped with a cabin, may be 35 to 45 feet in length, is powered either by a car or diesel engine, and is steered with a forward wheel. Of the five pinques which fish from the Ste. Marie wharf, two are owned by men living in the village. About twenty bateaux fish from this wharf; eleven of these bateaux are owned by Ste. Marie men.

The methods and equipment used in the inshore fishery are relatively common to all village fishermen. Navigational and emergency equipment are limited; all fishermen carry compasses in their boats, but maps or charts and emergency items such as flares or life-jackets are frequently absent. Most fishermen cannot swim, but villagers consider drowning as something that comes about because of carelessness or fate, that is, if someone inexplicably drowns it was his "time" to die. Villagers have ready examples to illustrate that knowing how to swim and carrying emergency equipment may have little relevance in influencing whether or not someone drowns.

The same kinds of equipment are used by all village fishermen in the lobster fishery. Custom regulates the size and construction of the wooden lath traps, but the law limits the number of traps permitted per lobster license to 375. Generally ten traps are attached to a line, forming a "jig" and each man sets his thirty or so "jigs" at various locations along the coast in rocky-bottom locations; traps are hauled and emptied each day and rebaited as necessary. A legal-size lobster, a minimum of two-and-one-half inches in carapace length, averages one to one-and-one-half pounds in weight; catching one lobster per trap is considered good fishing, with lobster to be canned or to be marketed fresh selling at 65¢ and 85¢ per pound, respectively (prices quoted are those of the summer of 1971). Depending on the season, a fisherman may not have more than one or two days in which he achieves an average of a lobster per trap. Occasionally a boat may bring in two or three thousand dollars worth of lobster in a week. However, in recent years it has become difficult for such large catches to be brought in consistently by one boat; overfishing is one reason catches for individual boats are small.

Groundfish, such as cod, plaice, and hake, are fished by trawl lines or nets; occasionally a fisherman prefers the use of a hand line, or "bob." A trawl line, several thousand feet in length and equipped with approximately five hundred hooks, is positioned near the ocean bottom. Each day the line (or lines) is pulled up by hand, the catch is removed, hooks are rebaited, and the line is reset. A cod net is 120 feet long and 12 feet wide; the nylon fiber mesh is four-and-one-half inches to six inches square in size.

Several nets are usually attached and set together near the ocean bottom. Each day, nets are hauled to the surface by hand (or by mechanical roller), the catch is removed, and the nets are reset.

A "bob" is a hand line with a shiny metal weight, shaped like a small mackerel, which contains two curved prongs or hooks. The "bob" is lowered near the ocean bottom and then jerked by hand; fish are attracted to the movement, or metallic glitter, of the head. Although this technique is time-consuming, several hundred pounds of fish per day can be caught with a "bob." Cod sells for 6¢ per pound and other types of groundfish, such as plaice, sell for 4¢ per pound. A minimally satisfactory catch is around 1,000 pounds per day.

Fall herring are also caught in nets. As herring are a pelagic species, the nets are set close to the surface of the water; the mesh opening is smaller to accommodate the smaller herring. Nets are pulled several times during the course of a fishing night, as opposed to being pulled once each day as for groundfish. The price received by fishermen varies according to whether the fall herring will be used for human consumption or will be processed into fish meal. Most fishermen also set nets for spring herring which are used as bait in the lobster fishery.

The Offshore Fishery

The offshore fishery is a large-scale, capital intensive enterprise; crews of at least three, and not usually more than a dozen, men undertake trips from several days to several weeks in duration in pursuit of groundfish, crab, or herring. Trips cover hundreds of miles with return to port (either Lameque, Shippegan town, or Caraquet) being determined by weather conditions or the completion of catches. Usually a vessel pursues one type of fish during a season; the species pursued may change from year to year depending on market demands and availability of runs.

Herring seiners may be gone several days or weeks on a fishing trip; their catch does not need processing on board ship as it will be made into meal on delivery at the usine. Groundfish and crab receive special handling and chilling to guard against spoilage. As the catch will be processed and packaged for human consumption at the usine, vessels fishing groundfish and crab must deliver the catch within a day or so after it is made to insure freshness.

Offshore fishing vessels vary considerably in size and elaborateness of equipment. Vessels owned by village men are between fifty and ninety feet in length and usually make fishing trips of only two to three days in duration. Some large offshore vessels are capable of remaining at sea for weeks, or even months; a few villagers have fished on such trawlers, which are usually owned by large companies rather than by individuals.

Offshore fishing is highly mechanized. Electronic equipment provides information on the location of fish, reading of the ocean bottom, and location of other vessels. Fish are caught in huge nets which the vessel either sets or drags through the water; machines haul or pump the catch into the ship. Crab are caught in large metal traps which are also set and hauled by machine. In effect, an offshore fisherman must know how to handle machinery as well as how to handle fish.

MAKING A LIVING 73

The offshore fishing season is longer than that of the inshore fishery, as the larger, more powerful offshore vessels can withstand the rough autumn and spring sea conditions; the offshore vessels generally fish a few weeks earlier and a month or so later than do inshore boats.

The annual incomes derived from the offshore fishery can be substantial. A man fishing on an offshore vessel receives a "share" for his wages. The usual arrangement is that 40 percent of the value of the catch is given to the owner of the boat; operating expenses (e.g., food, fuel, ice costs) are subtracted from the remaining 60 percent, and the remainder is then divided equally among crewmen, including the captain, each receiving his "share."

Captain-owners of fifty-foot offshore fishing vessels may have yearly net incomes of $10,000 to $15,000; crew members of herring seiners are reported to be able to make several hundred dollars a week. Such high wages for offshore fishermen are not assured, however, and depend on the season and particular experiences of the vessel. Many crew members probably do not earn incomes much larger than owners of inshore fishing boats. A study of the 1969 earnings of selected inshore and offshore fishermen in New Brunswick and Nova Scotia indicates that inshore fishermen earned slightly more than did crew members of offshore vessels fishing crab ($3,649: $3,639) and almost as much as crewmen on draggers fishing groundfish; within the offshore fishery earnings varied considerably according to the type and size of boat and the species pursued. Some captains of offshore fishing vessels earned several times the amount of crew members; their earnings also depend on the type and size of vessels owned and the species pursued (Charron 1972).

Within the village inshore fishery, incomes are modest; it is doubtful that any of the inshore boats brought in a seasonal catch exceeding $7,000 in 1971. This would entail the catch of $4,000 worth of lobster, or around 5,400 pounds at 75¢ per pound and $3,000 worth of groundfish, or 50,000 pounds at 6¢ per pound. Depending on the size of the crew (i.e., whether one, two, or three men fished in one boat for all or part of the season), gross incomes for most fishermen, as based on catches alone, would not have exceeded $3,500. According to official information on the value of catches landed at Ste. Marie in 1971, i.e., $50,000 worth of lobster, $31,000 worth of groundfish and $5,000 worth of herring (Environment Canada 1973), the average gross income per boat was around $3,500.

According to informants it is not easy to get positions on offshore vessels, and fishermen who gain entrance to the offshore fishery usually do not return to the inshore fishery. All but the youngest offshore fishermen began their fishing careers inshore and gradually worked their way into positions on offshore vessels. Consistently cited reasons for why individuals prefer offshore fishing include the easier working conditions and the higher wages, especially if one can become a captain on a vessel.

It is not easy to become a captain in the offshore fishery, but four of the sixteen offshore fishermen in Ste. Marie are captain-owners. To be a captain one must receive a "skipper's ticket," indicating the successful passing of special courses at the School of Fisheries in Caraquet. In order to buy a vessel one must secure a government subsidy and loan to partially cover its cost; this cost may run as high as a quarter-million dollars which is the price one villager paid for his vessel. The prospective buyer must supply a down payment equal to ten percent of the purchase price. The requirements of education, experience, and the ability to raise large amounts of capital, are not easily met by all men; hence, for many men achieving the position of captain-owner of an offshore vessel is only a remote possibility.

Village men fishing inshore or offshore live according to different daily and seasonal cycles of activity. Inshore fishermen work on a schedule that daily finds them at home with wife and children. Each day the wife sends her husband off with an early breakfast and expects him home for dinner (the noon meal), after which time he will be close to the house for the remainder of the day. All year long, inshore fishermen may be found in the village.

In the offshore fishery, men are absent from the village five days a week; they generally leave the village on Sunday afternoon, returning Tuesday, and leave again Wednesday afternoon to return on Saturday. Wives of captains commonly listen to ship-to-shore radio exchanges and hear their husbands converse with members of other ships, or report progress and location to the usines to which they sell their catches. Only indirectly, then, is the presence of offshore fishermen felt in their homes and in the village during much of the six to seven months fishing season.

However, inshore and offshore fishermen participate in the same yearly cycle of economic activity, alternating between "busy" or "dead." Together they work through the brief warm months of summer, each group of fishermen employing its special techniques for exploiting the ocean's wealth. Together they wait out the winter months, reminiscing over catches of past years and anticipating those of the coming year.

RELATIONSHIPS WITHIN ECONOMIC ACTIVITIES

Villagers have various kinds of occupations and participate in numerous economic relationships. I explore these relationships in order to understand the nature of village life in general and to gain insight into the channelling of relationships between villagers and Anglo-Canadians in economic fields. Discussion will be limited, however, to those economic and occupational relationships which are important in terms of the numbers of villagers who enter into them; these are the relationships which mainly stem from villagers' activities within the fishery, as members of crews, as buyers and sellers of fish, and as workers in usines.

Crews

The way in which crews are formed illustrates how contacts between villagers and Anglo-Canadians are minimized. The inshore fisheries of the North Atlantic coastal rim are characterized by the tendency for kinsmen, especially brothers, to make up substantial proportions of crews (Anderson and Wadel 1972); this pattern has been well described in the literature on the coastal fishery of Newfoundland (Faris 1966; Firestone 1967; Nemec 1972) and of the North Shore of the Gulf of St. Lawrence in Quebec (Charest n.d.; Breton 1973). Kin relations between crew members is a familiar phenomenon in Ste. Marie where, for at least part of the fishing season in 1971, half of the inshore fishing crews were made up of brothers, brothers-in-law, or double-first cousins. Individuals who were not related to other crew members were either residents of Ste. Marie or of other villages in St. Raphael Parish.

In the inshore fishery of Ste. Marie, the most enduring crew relationships, in terms of actual years spent fishing together, are those between fathers and sons and between brothers. Today, however, no village inshore fishing crew is made up of a father and son combination. This reflects several factors, the most important of which is that sons are no longer encouraged to enter the inshore fishery; rather they are encouraged to receive education or training that will give them entrance into other higher paying occupational fields.

Crews in the offshore fishery are also often composed of kin and friends or acquaintances; this is the case in Ste. Marie as well as in other areas of the North Atlantic coastal rim (Anderson and Wadel 1972b: 150-153). Only one of the sixteen offshore village fishermen does not work with a fellow villager or kinsman. Among kin relationships in these offshore fishing crews were two father-son dyads, two brother-brother dyads, and a triad composed of a villager and two brothers-in-law. Captains from Ste. Marie generally hire their crews from among village men, or from men living in other villages in St. Raphael Parish.

Thus crew members are known to each other in various roles--as fishermen, kinsmen, or neighbors. Sometimes kinsmen will purchase an offshore vessel together and operate the venture jointly; this has occurred in Ste. Marie in the past and is not uncommon in the Shippegan area as a whole. Thus, further roles--that of entrepreneur and joint-owner--may be added to the relationships between crewmen.

Generally, then, recruitment to offshore fishing crews follows kin and friend channels; brothers help younger brothers secure jobs and neighbors assist or hire neighbors looking for entrance to the fishery. An exceptional situation exists, however, in the recruitment of crews for herring seiners fishing from Caraquet, a port thirty miles from Lameque Island. Fishing on herring seiners, where the work is highly mechanized, living conditions comfortable, and the pay usually good, is preferred by many offshore fishermen; however, many herring seiners fishing from Caraquet are owned by firms from British Columbia and hire captains and crew from that province. Crew members are generally Anglo-Canadians and strangers to northeastern New Brunswick. Although four brothers from Ste. Marie did belong to crews on two of these vessels, it is reputed to be difficult for local men to get positions on the seiners. Crews on the British Columbian seiners fishing from Caraquet represent one of the few instances in which Acadians and Anglo-Canadians fish together.

There is local resentment toward the "B.C. seiners" which are felt to be "ruining the herring fishery on the East Coast just as they did on the West Coast." A few years ago, the wharf used by the seiners of one British Columbia firm was burned, supposedly by disgruntled people who wished to be rid of the seiners' presence in the area. That so few local men could gain positions on the seiners, or in the largely machine run <u>usine</u> which processed the fish into meal, was probably just as important a factor leading to the destruction of the wharf as were the conservationist attitudes among local people.

Within the fishery of the Shippegan area there are Anglo-Canadian fishermen from Miscou Island and elsewhere whose vessels use the Shippegan or Caraquet harbours. Nevertheless, recruitment in both the inshore and offshore fisheries generally follows lines of kinship and acquaintanceship so that crew relationships between Anglo-Canadians and villagers are rarely created.

Broker-fishermen

Owners of offshore fishing vessels are assigned by the government to supply fish to a particular local processing plant. Inshore fishermen are under no stipulation to sell fish to any particular <u>usine</u>. At the Ste. Marie wharf most fishermen sell their catch to either of two middlemen or brokers who transport and resell the catch to processing plants; one broker is from Ste. Marie and supplies fish to l'Association Coopérative des Pêcheurs de l'Île in Lameque; the other man is from another village in St. Raphael Parish and purchases fish for a private concern in Shippegan town, W. S. Loggie Company, Ltd.. All fish are sold fresh; villagers have not themselves processed fish prior to its marketing for several decades, contrary to the situation in Newfoundland where today inshore fishermen both supply and process groundfish prior to its sale.

Although kin and village ties between fishermen and broker are probably not unimportant in influencing to which man fish will be sold, the important factor is simply whether or not the fisherman is a member of the cooperative; if the man is not a co-op member, he has no alternative but to sell to the broker supplying Loggie's. A small processing shop in Ste. Marie purchases some groundfish from local fishermen, but because of the limited size of the operation it cannot absorb the quantities of fish caught by local men who might wish to sell to a plant other than the co-op.

Many households include members who participate in one of several local cooperatives or in the local Caisse-Populaire, a credit union. Many school children are enrolled in the Caisse-Scolaire; the largest grocery stores on the island and in St. Raphael Parish are both cooperatives. Nevertheless, some men prefer not to sell their fish to the cooperative in Lameque. Selling to the cooperative represents something of an investment for fishermen; less payment for fish is received by fishermen at the time of selling to the co-op broker than would be received from selling to the Loggie's broker, but an additional payment raising the return to a point higher than that received from Loggie's will be made at the end of the season if the cooperative has a profitable year. Some men remember years in which profits were not realized and additional payments were not made; as a result they severed ties with the fishermen's co-op and will not risk further involvement today. The merits of membership in any cooperative is a subject on which there is wide and sometimes heated disagreement among villagers. The co-op is presented as being of and for local people rather than being for the benefit of outsiders and strangers who

MAKING A LIVING   81

make the profits as in the other _usines_. Some villagers reject
this argument and suggest that even the co-op administrators are
not trustworthy and that in one way or another profits and dividends
may not be forthcoming as promised.

The Loggie enterprise was founded, and is still owned, by
Anglo-Canadians from the New Brunswick village of Loggieville. Not
many years ago, managerial positions in the Shippegan area Loggie
fish processing plants and store were reserved for Anglo-Canadians
who spoke French to varying degrees; the few Anglo-Canadian families
in Shippegan town today largely represent the remaining English-
speaking employees who came to the area as "Loggie people." For the
most part, this seems to have been a lonely "colonial" experience
for these Anglo-Canadians. Children were sent away to board where
they could attend English-language schools; wives did not learn
French and only mixed socially with each other, or occasionally,
with English-speaking people of Miscou; there were no churches,
clubs, or associations in which English was the working language.
The residence of an English-speaking Protestant minister in the
area during the summer months provided occasions for the Anglo-
Canadians to get together and, hence, was greatly anticipated.
Today the Anglo-Canadians with the Loggie Company are few; francophones from the area are usually hired to take over positions that
are vacated by the remaining Anglo-Canadians.

Although W. S. Loggie is an Anglo-Canadian company and has made
few concessions to the francophone milieu it serves (e.g., many
signs in the Loggie's general store in Shippegan town are written
in English), villagers do not voice objections to dealing with the

company. Daily contacts are not made with the Loggie Company per se, but are made with the broker who supplies the company.

The relationship between fishermen and their broker is a personal one in which the broker helps his fishermen in many small ways, such as bringing in bait from outside the area if local catches are small, loaning a truck to be used in hauling lobster traps to and from the wharf, and generally being friendly and helpful. The broker is officially recognized as the "employer" in the federal unemployment insurance scheme for fishermen; it is the broker who tallies the weekly value of catches which qualifies the fisherman for "stamps." It is the responsibility of the broker to insure that the fishermen receive the maximum amount of stamps due them. With the broker as an intermediary between fishermen and Loggie's, the important element in the relationship is that between fellow parishioners, villagers, or sometimes kinsmen, rather than between francophone fishermen and an Anglo-Canadian company.

That the relationship between fisherman and the receiver of his catch is fundamentally between fisherman and broker (rather than fisherman and company purchasing the fish) was underlined by events at the Ste. Marie wharf in 1973. Shortly before the opening of the fishing season, the broker supplying Loggie's suddenly decided that he would no longer provide the firm with fish; instead, he would supply a Shippegan company which heretofore had not purchased catches from fishermen of St. Raphael Parish. Loggie's lost nearly one-third of the total number of fishermen who had been supplying them because of the broker's action; it was said that the broker was receiving a higher commission from the new company than he had received from Loggie's. It was apparently of little import to fishermen where the catches were ultimately sold for they continued to hand over their catch to this particular broker. Loggie officials conceded that there was no need to send another representative to the Ste. Marie wharf for the fishermen would not switch their allegiance to a new broker.

Since the latter part of the eighteenth century the purchasing of fish in the Shippegan area has been largely done by Anglo-interests, either Anglo-Canadian, Anglo-American, or British companies. From an early period Channel Island firms, such as Robin and Company, served as intermediaries and supplied Shippegan people with goods in return for receiving their fish. Channel Islanders were bilingual and because of this language advantage had been favored to enter the area after the withdrawal of French companies at the end of the eighteenth century (Innis 1940: 187-92). Presumably representatives of other Anglo-companies in the area were bilingual as well. Nineteenth century Miscou Island fishermen, many of whom were of English origin, were dealing with the same fish-buying companies as the fishermen on Shippegan Island (Perley 1852); there is no indication that such Miscou people were bilingual, so I can only suggest that the brokers with whom they dealt were bilingual.

The bilingualism of these intermediaries, or brokers, provided convenience and ease of communication for local monolingual fishermen, and thus made it unnecessary for francophone fishermen to learn English or for anglophone fishermen to learn French. This situation can be contrasted with that reported in the Labrador fishing com-

munity of Blanc Sablon. In early years, Jerseymen or Channel
Islanders controlled much of the fishing industry there as they did
in the Shippegan area; however, these firms were eventually replaced
by the Hudson Bay Company which employed English monolinguals
(Junek 1937). As a result, residents of Blanc Sablon were forced
to use English in their dealings with the company, and, by so
doing, became bilingual; English was largely used in economic transactions and French was used in family and domestic life (Junek 1937:
105).

Men of Ste. Marie and the Shippegan area in general traditionally have been employed in primary industries which supplied raw,
or partially processed, products to largely Anglo-dominated companies based beyond the immediate area; however, the situation is
not parallel to those symbiotic arrangements elsewhere in the world
where different ethnic groups cooperate in producing or supplying
each other with specific kinds of goods or services (see Barth
1969a). In northeastern New Brunswick, and as close as on Miscou
Island, fishermen of English origins have played the same role as
supplier of products to Anglo-owned companies as have fishermen of
French origins on Lameque Island. The relationship between
suppliers of raw products and processors of these products has not
been one of French fishermen supplying Anglo-capitalists; rather it
has been one in which residents of the region, francophones and
anglophones, have supplied raw products to outside Anglo-owned
interests.

MAKING A LIVING   85

Usine Workers

With the exception of the small herring pickling plant and salted cod processing shop located in Ste. Marie, the usines in which villagers work are found either in Lameque or in Shippegan town. Though several of the usines are controlled by Anglo-Canadian or American interests, with the exception of the Loggie Company francophones hold local level management positions. Miscou Island's Anglo-Canadians find employment in several small fish processing shops on Miscou and on the north shore of Lameque Island.

A half dozen major usines provide work opportunities, and, thus, villagers find themselves working with kinsmen or with fellow parishioners. Villagers ride to work together and may even work side-by-side at the same worktable in the same usine. At the small village-based herring pickling plant, dozens of villagers, usually housewives and high schoolers on vacation, are employed a few weeks each year. Here, of course, relationships between workers are multiple, with ties of acquaintanceship, common village residence, and kinship being held by most workers.

Own-account Businesses in Ste. Marie

Villagers are not adverse to playing the role of entrepreneur. As noted earlier the following locally owned enterprises are found in Ste. Marie: three grocery stores, several rental chalets, a recreation center, a salted cod processing shop, an automobile repair shop, a sawmill, two independently owned gas pumps, and a foodstand.

None of these establishments represents the only source of in-

come for a particular individual or his household. Although wives
are commonly listed as owners of the businesses, the enterprises are
usually the joint ventures of husband and wife; moreover older
children are frequently entrusted with selling merchandise and wait-
ing on customers.

Economic Relationships and Social Life

In assessing the kinds of economic relationships which villagers
enjoy, it is useful to consider J. A. Barnes' distinction regarding
variation in mesh of social networks:

> one of the principal formal differences between simple,
> primitive, rural or small-scale societies as against
> modern, civilized, urban or mass societies is that in
> the former the mesh of the social network is small,
> in the latter it is large. By mesh I mean simply the
> distance round a hole in the network. In modern society,
> I think we may say that in general people do not have as
> many friends in common as they do in small-scale societies.
> When two people meet for the first time, it is rare in
> modern society for them to discover that they have a large
> number of common friends, and when this does happen it is
> regarded as something exceptional and memorable. In
> small-scale societies I think this happens more frequently,
> and strangers sometimes find that they have kinsmen in
> common (Barnes 1954:44).

Barnes considers Bremmes, a Norwegian island parish heavily dependent economically on the fishery, as representing an intermediate
society; that is, individuals in Bremmes are generally linked by
several social bonds, fewer bonds than might link those in a small-
scale society, but more than those linking individuals in a large-
scale society. So, too, would Ste. Marie be considered intermediate; within occupational or industrial-based fields individuals
play various roles to largely the same audience. This characteristic
of social life in Ste. Marie is encouraged by preferential hiring of

kinsmen and friends, by the existence of small family-owned and operated businesses, and by the limited opportunities in which villagers can seek employment. The intimacy of social life in the intermediate society undoubtedly encourages the maintenance of solidarity in crises; in Chapter Eight and the Appendix, I discuss how villagers and area residents cooperated in attacking a particularly serious problem of regional interest.

MAKING A LIVING: ADAPTATION IN STE. MARIE

Men in Ste. Marie usually have supplemental cash income in addition to that derived as fishermen or *usine* workers. The economic strategies of today's villagers can be usefully contrasted with those of villagers several decades ago and with those of Acadians residing elsewhere in the Maritime Provinces today.

Throughout the North Atlantic coastal rim, from eastern Canada to Scandinavia and the British Isles, there are certain features common to maritime communities. Of particular interest here is that rural maritime communities (as opposed to urbanized seaports) are generally characterized by diversified economic activities. That is, fishing has traditionally been but one part of a local economy which usually includes fishing and gardening and/or farming, both agriculture and animal husbandry. There is often a third economic activity which, in outports of Newfoundland, has been forestry or lumbering (Anderson and Wadel 1972a:1-3).

In some areas of the North Atlantic coastal rim, such economic diversity has diminished if not disappeared altogether (Rudie 1969/70), as has been the case in Ste. Marie. Prior to some thirty years ago, it was common in Ste. Marie for inshore fishermen to farm; they grew crops such as oats, barley, and potatoes, and raised sheep, pigs, cows, and various kinds of domestic fowl. Garden and animal products were used to fill household needs; surpluses, usually grain and potatoes, were marketed. In addition, some men followed a fall offshore fishery and fished cod from sail-driven schooners; during the winter some men worked in lumber camps for additional income. At this time no village men were involved full-time in the offshore fishery; until the early 1950s the New Brunswick offshore fishery was poorly developed and characterized by vessels and fishing techniques which had long before been discarded in other areas of the world (Gallagher 1955).

During the course of a year, an individual might have been a member of a local farmers' cooperative, a crew member of an offshore vessel fishing near Prince Edward Island, a member of a wood-cutting group working outside of Bathurst, and an inshore fisherman in Ste. Marie. Today participation in such wide-ranging and variously located economic activities has nearly disappeared. Although vegetable gardens are kept by many householders and some men own small woodlots, farming and lumbering are activities of the past for today's villagers. Similarly, only rarely will a man fish in both the inshore and offshore fisheries during the same year. The dependence by individuals on one main economic pursuit has drastically altered the kinds of economic networks in which villagers are involved. In some ways, an individual is more isolated socio-economically than was his father; the villager of several decades ago might rightfully have been able to claim acquaintanceship with most North Shore Acadian families, as well as many Anglo-Canadians, with whom he is related in some economic activity or another.

The traditional economic adaptation, or strategy, by which villagers of the past simultaneously, or over the course of a year, held several occupations can be described as "pluralistic." Comitas has defined occupational plurality or multiplicity as "a condition wherein the modal adult is systematically engaged in a number of gainful activities which form for him an integrated economic complex" (1963:41). Occupational plurality has been described as one response to a situation in which no single economic activity can provide an adequate income, and thus one follows a number of marginally productive activities which in combination will provide an acceptable, if perhaps minimum, income (Comitas 1963:44). In Ste. Marie the disappearance of the traditional triad of occupational roles (i.e., fisherman-farmer-woodsman) held by village men was a response to change within the fishery itself (including improved fish prices, the creation of a cash market, the eligibility of fishermen for unemployment insurance payments), as well as the generally depressed economy in northeastern New Brunswick which continues to discourage the securing of winter work by villagers.

As noted above, however, many working adults of the village, especially males, have two or more sources of income (exclusive of household income derived from various social assistance schemes). Typical combinations of economic activities include (with that occupation listed first which the individuals themselves identified as their occupations): Pierre T.--inshore fisherman, boat maker; Jean R.--<u>usine</u> worker, carpenter; Raymond L.--storekeeper, owner of rental property; Re-Jean L.--school bus driver, cod fisherman, owner of rental property; Jacques P.--buyer of fish (broker), _usine_ worker, storekeeper.

Not all adults have more than one source of income; villagers with better paying jobs, non-seasonal workers and offshore fishermen, usually have only one income source. Villagers making lower incomes, such as inshore fishermen and _usine_ workers, are those most likely to engage in several economic activities. As in the Caribbean (Comitas 1963), the holding of several occupations in Ste. Marie is a function of age and marital status; those who engage in multiple economic activities are married men with several children. It would appear that as lower-paid villagers' responsibilities increase, the number of gainful activities in which they are engaged also increases.

Each man's combination of economic activities may be described as individualized. The same activities may be carried out by others in the village, but an individual's combined activities are unique to him. In Ste. Marie each man creates his own special strategy by which he has one extra-village trade or business to conduct in the outside world and another (or several others) to follow within the village context. The various activities will depend on the freedom given him by his primary economic pursuit (e.g., free time provided in the dead season), his own interests and skills, and special social advantages, such as ties with kin or neighbors who may assist him. Thus, for example, one man drives a school bus ten months of the year (September-June), fishes groundfish with his brother two months (July-August), and, with the help of his wife and children, maintains and rents shore cottages. As each man pursues his own strategy of multiple economic activities, there is less "competition for scarce strategic resources within a finite area" than in the Caribbean situation described by Comitas (1963:47).

The primary source of income for most villagers comes from labor performed outside of the village; supplementary sources of income derive from activities conducted in the village. There are few, if any, area jobs for which villagers qualify during the dead season; jobs such as wood-cutting are reported to pay less than unemployment insurance payments, and villagers rationally retain their rights to unemployment payments by not taking such wage labor. Nevertheless, within the relative safety of the village and within the confines of their own homes or property, individuals are quick to consider various personal-specific schemes by which they may earn varying amounts of cash (e.g., providing taxi service, selling fish and vegetable produce, making and selling lobster traps to tourists and fishermen); such unreported earnings do not endanger one's status as a recipient of unemployment payments. It is in this realm that the innovation, energy, and hard work of many villagers are most evident, though the returns accrued may be individually quite small. Hence, for every one source of income reported by villagers, they may also have one or two additional sources providing small amounts of cash.

This particular kind of economic adaptation is of considerable importance in understanding not only the villagers' approach to economic survival, but in understanding Acadian survival as a whole. Acadians have been forced to be flexible to survive since the eighteenth century when they traded simultaneously with French at Louisbourg, English in Halifax, and New Englanders across the Bay of Fundy, while also remaining on friendly terms with local Indians. Today's economic activities in Ste. Marie may be considered merely a further reflection of this kind of flexibility.

A rare economic adaptation in Ste. Marie is the year-long absence of men who work elsewhere and who return to visit wife and children on weekends or at less regular intervals. Only two men, a man and his son, are currently engaged in labor of this sort. Occasionally a young man with construction skills or a trade may be hired for several months labor elsewhere in Canada; a few village men have worked intermittently in Labrador where wages are high. Going to relatively distant places such as Labrador is only done on a temporary basis and usually for the specific purpose of saving enough money to build or buy a house in the village.

Some Acadians in Nova Scotia regularly work outside of their home villages and return to these villages on weekends. These Acadians come from rural areas in which lumbering and farming were important, but, with reduced returns from these activities, villagers have turned to the more profitable wage labor in urban industrial centers (Tremblay 1966). Traditionally such urban centers have been dominated by anglophones and in this context, then, Acadians are said to increasingly adopt the use of English and undergo acculturation.

If year-long factory or plant jobs were available in northeastern New Brunswick, villagers might attempt commuting to such work as do those Acadians in Nova Scotia who commute between village and industrial centers. However, New Brunswick's road and transportation system is not good and the industrial climate has not been consistently healthy in northeastern New Brunswick. The regional pulp and paper industry and the mining and smelting operations that operate on an annual basis have not prospered in recent years; reduction, rather than expansion, of the work force has been the rule.

In sum, the depressed regional economy and the relatively improved position of those in the fishery and related secondary industry have combined to inhibit men from seeking work beyond the village.[1] Thus potential inter-ethnic group contacts in work situations beyond the area have been discouraged.

Opportunities for economically-based contacts between villagers of Ste. Marie and Anglo-Canadians are obviously limited by the absence of a large Anglo-Canadian work force in the Shippegan area. However, I have suggested that the physical isolation of villagers from Anglo-Canadians does not entirely account for the lack of such contacts. Rather, I have found that sociocultural processes, such as those involved in crew formation and the intermediation by bilingual brokers, discourage the creation of occupational ties that could be made between villagers and locally-based Anglo-Canadians.

The next chapter also focuses on the processes by which contacts between villagers and Anglo-Canadians are minimized by considering the ways in which Anglo-Canadians are excluded from villagers' domestic lives, as reflected in patterns relating to kinship, marriage, and residence.

PATTERNING CONTINUITY: KINSHIP

In studies of French Canadians in Nova Scotia and Quebec, it has been demonstrated that family and domestic life are important factors influencing the development of bilingualism, English language adoption, and the acculturation of French Canadians. It has been found that if a French Canadian is married to either a bilingual or monolingual English Canadian, the French Canadian is prone to adopt English for daily use within the home and for reception of communications media (television, magazines); also, children of mixed marriages are apt to learn English as a first language (Carisse 1971; Tremblay 1961).

In Ste. Marie there are no mixed marriages and, thus, English language adoption is not encouraged in domestic or familial contexts. In this chapter I discuss factors which influence mate selection; I focus on kinship and kin role behavior. I discuss two major kin categories (famille and parenté), the behavior expected of specific types of kin, and residence and household composition. A final section sums up important criteria in selecting mates.

RECKONING OF FAMILLE AND PARENTÉ

If it is the ocean and the fishery which serve as a backdrop against which village life unfolds, it is in the web of kinship that individual lives unfold. Within the context of family life, stages of individual development and maturity are achieved; it is with one's kin that lifelong relationships are enjoyed or, in some cases, simply endured; it is by performance as kinsman and family member that villagers judge each other.

Villagers largely categorize people as being kinsmen, neighbors, or strangers. Thus, as in many areas of the world, to be able to claim kin ties with others is of considerable importance. The major kin categories recognized by villagers are famille and parenté, which roughly correspond to the terms "family" and "relatives" used by anglophones throughout North America. Famille includes members of the kin groups anthropologically known as the family of orientation and the family of procreation; this kin category also includes grandparents, grandchildren, and various affines. Individuals other than famille with whom one claims kinship, either consanguineously or affinally, are parenté.

There is a lack of consistency in the use of the terms "family" and "relatives" by North Americans (Schneider 1968) and of famille and parenté by villagers. I attempt to use the terms famille and parenté as villagers do, but the distinction between the two is not always clear for all villagers, i.e., not all informants agreed on which kin statuses belong to each category. In the more ambiguous instances, whether or not an individual is considered famille or parenté is determined by specific features of the relationship, such as if the individual has lived in close proximity to Ego and if there has been a continuing relationship between the two. Although the boundaries of the two kin categories are not always clear, the distinction between the two categories has relevance for villagers, as discussed in the following pages.

FAMILLE

The kin category famille includes parents, children, spouse, siblings and their spouses, grandparents, grandchildren, and the spouse's parents, grandparents, siblings and their spouses. In this discussion I focus on the most important and generally recognized kin types within famille--parents and children, siblings, and spouses.

Parents and Children

I begin this discussion by considering the relationship between parents and children in Ste. Marie. As elsewhere, the relationship between parents and children entails affection and obligation. Affection that villagers hold for their children and parents is lifelong; the specific obligations held as parent or child alter during the life cycle.

Generally the father's primary duty is to provide for his children; he must try to earn a good salary with which to feed, clothe, and shelter his family. The duty of the mother is to take care of the children--to teach them good behavior and their prayers, prepare their food, provide clothes and keep them clean, and generally make a good home for the children.

In turn, children are expected to perform various household chores (to wash dishes, run errands, take care of younger siblings, and generally assist their parents) and to do their school work.

KINSHIP   97

Children are encouraged to stay in school; education is viewed as a means to obtaining better paying jobs. It is not uncommon for children to fail to pass a grade or to drop out of school, and thus parents are particularly proud when a child graduates from high school or obtains additional training beyond the secondary school level.

As a result of caring for younger children, girls have learned a great deal about rearing a family by the time they are ready to do so themselves. Similarly, in the past fathers taught their sons much, if not all, that the boys needed to know to provide for their own future families; today this is not so. Much of the inshore fishermen's knowledge and skills is not relevant to the needs of their sons, many of whom will become teachers, hospital orderlies, construction workers, or <u>usine</u> workers.

Parental obligations to provide for the child are completed when the child marries; a final obligation is the providing of a suitable wedding celebration for the child, which may involve the spending of hundreds of dollars. Parents also give expensive parties to celebrate the entrance of a son or daughter into a religious order. If possible, parents will always help a son or daughter in time of need. For example, if housing is difficult to obtain, one or more young married children, their spouses, and children may move in with the old parents for a short time.

Grown children, especially those who live within the area, have an important duty to remain in frequent contact with their parents, either in person or by phone; over half of the village household heads have parents who also live in Ste. Marie and contacts between these villagers and their parents take place daily. If an adult child neglects to visit his parents for several days, his parents might ask him if he has been "on a trip" since he has not been seen for so long. Children who have moved away to other areas usually return each summer to visit their parents. Visiting and enjoying one's children and grandchildren in one's old age are reasons villagers give to justify having children; villagers believe that someone who has no children will suffer greatly from loneliness.

If parents become quite old and physically incapacitated, they may move in with a married child and his family. However, if an old couple enjoy reasonably good health and are able to look after themselves, they will continue to live alone and be quite independent although reliant on their children for transportation to church or stores. In general, oldsters in good health do not ask for help in strenuous or even dangerous tasks; hardy oldsters of ninety row boats near the shore and haul driftwood for firewood; men of near eighty repair chimneys on their two story houses and continue to participate in the lobster fishery.

The Catholic Church stresses the importance and sacredness of the family; the respect and honor due parents and the value of having children are emphasized in sermons and in celebrations of special feast days or holidays, such as Mother's Day, when a party at the community center is given for all the mothers of the parish. Thus, the relationship between parents and children is defined and reinforced in local religious activities.

Siblings

Although the relationship between siblings is perhaps not as intense as that between parents and children, the relationship is more long lasting. Many villagers live their entire lives in close proximity to their siblings; about 80 percent of the household heads have siblings who also head village households.

Large numbers of children per family are common in the village and, from birth, the relationship between siblings is strong and largely positive. The importance of sibling ties is symbolized by the frequency with which youngsters are made the baptism or confirmation sponsors of their younger brothers and sisters. Later, in adulthood, new parents often ask their siblings and siblings' spouses to be the baptism or confirmation sponsors of their own children.

As youngsters, siblings work and play together; siblings of like age and the same sex are found together more than those of opposite sex or those in which much age difference lies between them. As children mature, they are entrusted with the care of their smaller brothers and sisters, and they may take care of them for hours at a time--playing with them, feeding them, and reprimanding them. Children of ten or eleven are given their small siblings of one or two years of age to take on wagon rides or to carry around and entertain while the mother is otherwise engaged. Older children often help their brothers and sisters with homework and lessons.

In families including ten or twelve children, childbearing may have been spread over twenty or thirty years. Hence, the older children mature, marry, and establish households and families of their own while their younger siblings remain at home. These young siblings often become the playmates of their older brothers' and sisters' children, or, if these young siblings are old enough, they frequently become baby-sitters of their nieces and nephews. Older wage earning children often give gifts or money to parents, items which directly or indirectly serve to make the home life of the younger siblings more comfortable. Hence, the large age difference between siblings does not hinder or impede their contact, but may even encourage affection and the creation of obligations.

When siblings grow up and prepare for their weddings, two may choose the same date and, thus, have their marriages performed in a _mariage_ _double_. Marriages in which the sibling of a woman marries a sibling of the woman's husband are not rare in the village or area as a whole; siblings involved in such marriages usually have a particularly strong relationship involving frequent visiting.

Between adult siblings an important obligation is caring for each other's children in crises. If one or both parents die or become incapacitated, siblings of the parents usually will care for the children, sometimes for years or until the children have reached maturity.

Adult siblings often establish households on adjoining pieces of land; as a result, visiting and contact between siblings' households may be daily and casual. As in the past, it is common for brothers to fish together at some time in their lives; today four pairs of brothers fish all or part of the season together in the inshore fishery.

In general then, many people pass their lives in close proximity to one or more of their siblings. Perhaps in fishing together, perhaps in sharing land boundaries, certainly in visiting and sharing events and celebrations together, siblings remain important to each other throughout their lives.

Spouses

Marriage is inevitable for most villagers. Within the village, there are five men past the age of thirty and only one woman over twenty-five who have never married, but only the religious celibate and the physically or mentally handicapped are expected to remain unmarried.

Today, unlike the past, parental approval of a marriage partner is not necessary before a wedding takes place. Although some parents claim they would not interfere with the choice of a child's marriage partner (whether the individual selected was French or English, Acadian or Quebecker, Catholic or Protestant), with the exception of one spouse from Quebec, all marriages in the village are between Acadians. Marriage partners usually come from the village or its immediate area. Of the village's sixty-six marital units, only 11 involve villagers and non-islanders; another 16 marriages involve a villager and someone from another island parish; 16 more marriages are between a villager and someone from another village in St. Raphael Parish; and in 23 marriages both partners are from Ste. Marie. Thus, only 17 percent of the marriages in the village contain partners who originate off the island, and the majority of marriages are between persons from the village and parish.

In Ste. Marie the primary duty of the conjugal unit is to produce children. Once the children start arriving, many of the duties and obligations that spouses have toward each other derive from their role as parents. Thus, the analytic separation of responsibilities held as mother or wife and as father or husband is difficult to make.

A woman generally expects her spouse will conduct himself respectably and soberly; village women often praise the virtues of their husbands by saying that their men neither get drunk nor chase women. If a husband is expected to be faithful and steady in his marital obligations, the wife is expected to be faithful and fertile. Many women become pregnant within a short period following marriage. Forty of the seventy-one married women in the village were pregnant in their first year of marriage. Since information on miscarriages was not obtained, the number of pregnancies might even be higher than this. If the wife is working and the young married couple is attempting to save money for house and furniture, the couple is not under pressure to begin a family immediately. Not ever wanting children, however, is something that villagers attribute only to les anglais.

If one spouse should die, the other, especially if a male, will remarry. Men are reputed to find remarrying necessary in order to satisfy their sexual needs. An oldster from a neighboring village remarried at the age of some eighty years. The girl he married was less than twenty and, within a year of marriage, she had borne a child, reported to have been that of her husband. Though villagers consider this an unusual situation, they accept it as an example of how men retain their sexual prowess and needs long into old age.

It is not unusual for a man to remarry relatively soon after losing a spouse. However, if he remarries within less than a year of his wife's death, he is liable to become a subject of gossip for having forgotten her. The first-born child of a second marriage will often be named after the first spouse and, thus, the deceased spouse will not be forgotten.

Widowers with children must remarry relatively quickly or face the break-up of their family. This seems to stem from the sexual division of labor. The special realm of women is the home and garden. The woman's responsibility is to keep the home and family in good order and to provide much of the care and attention needed by children. With the death of his wife, the husband is hard-pressed to care for the home and children and maintain a job at the same time.

Widows, in contrast, can continue with household and garden chores while caring for young children and, hence, they have a better chance of keeping the family together. The success of such attempts can vary in the village. Three such widows managed to rear their children and provided for them through limited farming and gardening or by securing wage labor. On the other hand, another widow and her children are reported to have survived only through the generosity and charity of kinsmen and neighbors.

In general, responsibility for important decision-making within the family rests with the husband-father. In some contexts, however, women have a hand in making decisions. For example, women are responsible for selecting purchases for the home and children. The increased importance of women as wage earners has undoubtedly enlarged their role in decision-making. The husband's and wife's combined income, both wages and unemployment insurance payments, has allowed many families to increase their material well-being and to encourage the children to stay in school.

In years past young boys left school to begin fishing with their fathers, and girls generally received a few more years formal education than did boys. As a result, many village women are better educated than their husbands.

Today women assume active roles in church and school activities. Women are frequently elected to leadership positions on parish committees, and wives usually represent their families at formal gatherings which relate to church and school. Groups or committees which deal with economic and political affairs, such as the Chambre de Commerce, commonly derive their membership from parish males; hence, there is a division of interest between wives and husbands regarding community as well as domestic activities.

The nature of the relationship between specific wives and husbands depends on features such as the age, education, and wage earning capacity of the individuals involved. However, even when young wives earn wages and have more education than their husbands, males appear to retain the authority and dominance in the marital and familial unit. Many daily activities do not require the villager's ability to read or write well, and, for at least several years, women remain at home to take care of small children. Hence, only at certain times during the life cycle do women contribute income to the household and only intermittently do women supply an educational skill their husbands may need.

In sum, the relationships between parents and children, siblings and spouses are the most important ones in which villagers are involved. With spouse and siblings, villagers share obligations of work and cooperation; to parents and children, villagers must give care and attention. Other members of the famille (grandchildren, grandparents, and in-laws) vary in importance; villagers interact more frequently with those of the famille who live in the village or parish than with those who live elsewhere. Although their interaction does not always stem from kin-related activities, the ties between kinsmen are maintained, if not strengthened, by frequent contact. This is so with regard to famille as well as parenté, the group which is described next.

PARENTÉ

Parenté are kinsmen who, though not themselves members of Ego's famille, are related to some member of Ego's famille and, hence, are related to Ego. Among these kinsmen are uncles, aunts, nieces, nephews, and cousins whom I collectively term core parenté. The obligations between core parenté are those connected with special events and the celebration of life crises. Thus, the combined group of famille and core parenté approximates what Murdock has defined as the kindred: "that group of near kinsmen who may be expected to be present and participant on important ceremonial occasions, such as weddings, christenings, funerals, Thanksgiving and Christmas dinners, and 'family reunions'" (1949:56-57). In life crises, one has the right to request or expect the attendance and assistance of famille and core parenté. Correspondingly, these kinsmen have an obligation to behave according to the requirements of the situation; and they have a right to expect reciprocal behavior sometime in the future.

Visiting parenté is not an obligation as it is with famille; rarely does one visit parenté who live outside of one's neighborhood. Once an individual reaches adulthood and marries, he will seldom visit many members of his core parenté, even though they live in the same village. Thus, outside of life crises, villagers may have little direct contact with many core parenté; information about each other is largely passed through intermediaries such as other kinsmen.

There are no commonly used terms for kin statuses beyond the second ascending or descending generation, nor beyond the second-degree collateral range. Villagers do not consider it necessary to have terms for more distantly related kinsmen; life spans are seldom long enough to enable an individual to know these kinsmen and specific terms for them are unnecessary. Similarly, although individuals related to Ego in a third-degree collateral range may live in the village, there is little, if any, interaction between Ego and such relatives along kinship lines. Such persons are known as villagers or neighbors, rather than as a specific type of parenté, or in some cases are not referred to as parenté at all.

A great many of the villagers and area residents could claim themselves as parenté. However, each individual also normally has many members of his famille in the area. Obligations and interest in members of famille are set before those connected with parenté, and, hence, interaction with parenté is necessarily limited.

KINSHIP

The importance of _parenté_, with whom there may be only vague recognition and negligible interaction, lies in the nature of the kin category itself. _Parenté_ kin ties are extensive and diffuse; _parenté_ provide a buffer zone, as it were, for Ego and his _famille_ against the outside world of strangers. On initially meeting someone, the first order of business for villagers is to investigate the possible kin ties that the individual may share with the villager; the purpose is to verify that there is indeed some relationship, be it ever so tenuous and distant, and that the individual is not a stranger.

HOUSEHOLD AND RESIDENCE

Patterns of household composition and residence have altered over the last few decades in response to changing economic adaptations of villagers, but household composition and residence remain important factors encouraging close ties between kinsmen.

Almost 60 percent of the 71 village households are composed of nuclear families; village households nearly always correspond to some collection of kinsmen. Variation in household composition largely represents different stages in a family and/or household development cycle. Residence is ideally neolocal; the initial and final stages of the household cycle comprise a husband and wife and the middle stage includes husband, wife and children. It is not unusual, however, for a newly married couple to live with one set of parents for up to a year or so, nor is it unusual for older villagers to live with their married children. Such living arrangements are similar to those historically found in the village, though the bases for the contemporary and historical patterns are quite different.

The Household Of The Recent Past

Prior to twenty-five or thirty years ago, the domestic cycle through which villagers passed reflected an adaptation in which household members engaged in diversified economic activities; some of these activities were for subsistence purposes only while others were for the acquisition of credit at local stores. Entire households cooperated in these activities: men fished, processed their catch, and farmed; boys helped with various chores and also became "helpers" in the fishery at the age of twelve or thirteen; women and girls were responsible for drying the salted cod, took care of gardens and farm animals, and performed a multiplicity of household chores.

Marriages took place at an early age when the man was perhaps nineteen or twenty and the woman a year or two younger. The first few years of married life were commonly spent in the husband's father's house. Some village houses were built specifically to accommodate two families; sleeping quarters were separate, but a kitchen-living area was shared. On at least one occasion such a house was eventually cut in two and moved apart when friction among the householders demanded it. When two nuclear families inhabited the same house, there was only one household. That is, the men cooperated in fishing and farming; the women cared for the house, garden, and processed fish; and there was a joint "household purse."

In effect, the earnings and the labor of the younger couple were invested in the parental house and property which the younger couple would inherit if they stayed on in the house. The responsibility of caring for the parents in their old age would also fall to the young couple inheriting the homestead.

It was not always the eldest son who remained in the house and eventually inherited the property. If there was a ready supply of maturing sons with whom the parent could fish and farm, the young conjugal unit would be encouraged to establish its own household and to begin fishing and farming independently. At that time, another son was usually ready to step in as his father's helper, to marry, and to bring home a wife to his father's house.

If the father owned an abundant amount of land, each son would receive land on which to build a house and farm, and to use as a base for fishing. If land was limited, the eldest son might receive a piece of land and the son remaining at home to fish with the father received the balance of the family land, house, and fishing equipment when the father died or retired.

There might have been several sons who obtained land either by purchasing it or by marrying someone who was given land by her parents. These young men could fish with older men who had no sons of a suitable age to act as helpers, or with brothers who themselves had no sons old enough to assist them.

In the past, then, households frequently comprised an extended family, sometimes containing three generations (the old parents and a younger conjugal unit with their children), and other times two generations only (two brothers and their nuclear families). The development cycle through which households passed usually included a stage in which three generations of a family were present. In some cases, individuals might have lived most of their lives in a three-generation household.

The traditional domestic cycle was influenced by several factors: 1) a large adult household work force, composed of men and women, was useful in carrying out the diversified economic activities; 2) as the selling of fish and agricultural products was done for credit, not for cash, it was an advantage for a man to have unpaid helpers in his son and in the son's wife; 3) it was difficult to accumulate cash savings to begin domestic life in an independent household or to sustain oneself after retirement and when in ill health; thus it was advantageous to earn the right to land, property, and equipment as a young married couple, and to be assured care in old age by having the right to award the household property to a child remaining at home.

The Contemporary Household

Today the need for a large household work force has diminished. Fish are sold fresh and not processed by the fishermen, and, with the advent of trap haulers, lobster fishing--the most important fishery for village men--can be satisfactorily carried out with the labor of one man. Farming ceased to be of importance over thirty years ago and now only a few villagers keep domestic fowl, and many villagers do not even maintain a vegetable garden. With the creation of a cash market for fish by 1940, sons serving as their fathers' helpers began demanding wages for their labor, rather than the promise of inheritance. With this cash, they were earlier able to establish their own households, independent of those of their fathers. With cash savings and the receipt of old age pensions, older villagers gained the financial freedom to live their retirement years independently of their children. Finally, increased work opportunities, some of which provided higher wages than those earned in inshore fishing, encouraged employment outside of that fishery. Current cases in which members of a young conjugal unit live permanently with parents (and stand to inherit land and property) are those in which a parent would be otherwise living alone or is in poor health; no married son lives and works with his father today.

Residence Selection

The place of birth of marital partners strongly influences where villagers will take up residence. Information on the current place of residence of married children of thirty-three households indicates that 46 percent of those who married someone from the village have set up households in the village (nine males and nine females out of a total of thirty-nine individuals); about 97 percent of the children who reside outside the village have non-villagers as spouses (76 out of 78). Thus, data covering individuals who have married during approximately the last forty years indicate that neither sons nor daughters are any more prone than the other to set up residence in the village; rather, residence is dependent upon whether one or both of the marriage partners were born in Ste. Marie.

Ste. Marie is relatively closed to the establishment of households by individuals who are not originally from the village. Only three permanently maintained households are headed by persons who were not born in Ste. Marie.

Access to property in Ste. Marie has remained closed to non-villagers, not because all property is handed down in families through inheritance or gift, but because the availability of land and property is usually made known privately, with relatives and then neighbors having first opportunity to make purchases; hence, properties have remained in the hands of villagers. Today in the Shippegan area there is a demand for houses, lots for houses and mobile homes, and shore frontage for cottages. Some villagers have begun considering the sale of land to individuals from beyond the village and parish, and outsiders' access to village land may increase in coming years.

As mentioned earlier, householders are related to many other residents of the neighborhood; residence is usually established in the neighborhood in which one of the villagers has originated. That is, if either the male or female heading the household (i.e., actual household head or spouse of the head) originally came from the village, residence will usually be set up in the neighborhood from which that member of the marital unit came; if both members are from the same neighborhood, residence will always be set up in that neighborhood. When members are of different neighborhoods in the village, residence is set up more often in the neighborhood of the male than of the female (Table III). These kin-based neighborhoods appear to be similar to "core neighborhoods" described in the Newfoundland community of "Island Harbour" (Stiles 1972:43).

Table III

Origin of Heads of Households, Residence in Ste. Marie, and Means of Household Land Acquisition

		Land acquired from		
		Husband's Parents	Wife's Parents	Bought
A. Husband only from Ste. Marie				
Residence: Husband's neighborhood	25	16	--	9
Other neighborhood	5	1	--	4
	30	17		13
B. Wife only from Ste. Marie				
Residence: Wife's neighborhood	10	--	4	6
Other neighborhood	2	--	1	1
	12		5	7
C. Husband and Wife from same neighborhood				
Residence: Same neighborhood	18	8	2	8
Other neighborhood	--	--	--	--
	18	8	2	8
D. Husband and Wife from different neighborhoods				
Residence: Husband's neighborhood	6	3	--	3
Wife's neighborhood	1	--	1	--
Other neighborhood	1	--	--	1
	8	3	1	4
Totals	68*	28	8	32

*An additional three households are situated on land purchased by a conjugal unit in which neither the husband nor the wife were from Ste. Marie originally.

Although the dimensions of the household group in Ste. Marie have decreased in terms of members and generations, a wide range of kin remains important and, as it were, resists dispersal by concentrating their residence in the neighborhood. In earlier times, one household made up of many members was situated on one piece of land; today that piece of land has been carved up through inheritance or sale and now may hold several kin-related households. Each household may have fewer members than a household of thirty or forty years ago, but the total number of persons in all the households on that piece of land exceeds that of the single household of the past. Reduction in the size of the kin group residing in a single household does not necessarily indicate that kinsmen today are less strongly attached in affection and interaction than in the past. As nearly half of the household properties have been purchased rather than inherited, these residence locations reflect choice and desire on the part of villagers to live close to kinsmen, especially to members of the famille.

MATE SELECTION

The preceding description of kin roles and behavior, household composition, and residence patterns suggests the importance of kin relationships in Ste. Marie. Maintaining good relations with kinsmen insures that one gets along with a great number of one's neighbors as neighbors are often also kinsmen. Consequently, the selection of a mate is an important matter, for the mate selected may facilitate or impede one's attempts to get along with others in the village.

KINSHIP   115

Generally villagers choose local Acadians to be their mates; all marriages but one were formed with fellow Acadians, and 83 percent of the unions involve marriage with fellow islanders. I next discuss some aspects relating to the importance of local and ethnic origins in the selection of mates.

Local Origins

The small universe from which villagers have selected mates largely reflects the restricted area in which villagers interact and in which they may meet potential mates. For many villagers the world of social interaction stretches no further than Lameque Island where they are provided with education, religious services, health care, employment, shopping, and entertainment. The importance of the bridge connecting the island and the mainland lies not so much in allowing villagers daily access to the mainland world, but in making mainland goods, services and jobs more conveniently available as needed and in triggering growth on the island. With continued economic and social expansion on the island (as reflected in the opening of a drive-in theatre and a sports arena, the enlarging of previously existing peat moss plants and fish processing usines, and the building of new plants and usines), the mainland is perhaps no more necessary to villagers than it was before the construction of the bridge.

In addition to their limited opportunities for meeting individuals from beyond the parish and island, villagers hold negative views about non-islanders, both Anglo-Canadian and Acadian. There has long been a history of less than amiable relations between residents of Lameque Island and those of the mainland town of Shippegan. Jealousy and suspicion characterize the attitudes of islanders toward those of the mainland; Shippegan people are said to have not wanted the bridge built to the island as "they never want people on the island to have anything"; the recent selection of locations for schools to be shared by mainlanders and islanders provided occasions for reopening old animosities as each group attempted to win the new schools for their own areas. Although the bridge is convenient for villagers working at mainland usines, and for others wishing to visit relatives and friends or to go to dances in Shippegan town or elsewhere on the mainland, the bridge is not seen by villagers of Ste. Marie as valuable in providing opportunities to get to know mainlanders better. One villager suggested that only after the bridge was built did rough, troublesome strangers start appearing on the island, and now villagers find it necessary to lock their doors when they are out lest some stranger rob them in their absence.

Thus, limited opportunities for meeting, and negative views held toward, non-islanders have combined to discourage villagers from marrying people from beyond the island. However, the recent consolidation of secondary schools and the bringing together of students from various parts of the civil parish may contribute to increasing the numbers of marriages between mainlanders and islanders in the future.

Correspondingly villagers have positive attitudes about marrying someone of local origins. Because of the frequent interaction among, and obligations toward, kinsmen, there is a decided advantage in marrying someone from the immediate area--someone who fits in if help and cooperation must be given to kinsmen, and someone who has kinsmen close by who can be called in time of need.

If individuals from the parish marry, it is not uncommon for some prior kin relationship to exist between the two. Traditionally the Catholic Church attempted to limit the degree of consanguinity between marriage partners. Until some twenty years ago, the degree of consanguineal relationship between partners was noted in the parish registry; a fee was collected in order to process the request for dispensation from regulations forbidding marriages between relatives. Today the only marriage between consanguines which is officially discouraged (other than incestuous ties between members of a nuclear family) is between first cousins. A small fee is still collected to cover the paperwork entailed in obtaining Church approval of such a marriage.

Marriage between first cousins is rare, however, and marriages between parenté usually involve distantly related kinsmen. Such individuals do not marry as a result of affective ties having been formed from contact as kinsmen. Rather, parenté who marry have rarely known each other as specific kinsmen (such as second cousin), although they may have known that they were related. The existence of prior kin ties smooths the way for parental acceptance of the marriage, but does not bring about the conditions in which such attraction is initially created or encouraged. In addition, marrying someone who is parenté enables one more rapidly to form close relationships with in-laws. For example, the use of the familiar terms mémère and pépère, sometimes used to refer to (and to address) mother-in-law and father-in-law respectively, are reported by informants to be adopted more quickly in situations in which Ego had parenté bonds with his in-laws prior to his marriage.

Ethnic Origins

Marrying someone of local origins is usually highly desirable. Knowing, and being known in, the area are positive features which allow individuals to fit into village life. Nevertheless, within the civil parish live a few hundred Anglo-Canadians, and villagers do not marry these people for ethnic origins are ultimately more important than local origins in influencing mate selection.

Acadians have long been encouraged to marry fellow Acadians in order to keep their language, religion, and culture pure. A factor which has traditionally insured that Acadians did not marry Anglo-Canadians was the Catholic Church's discouragement of mixed marriages. In New Brunswick few francophones are not at least nominally Catholic, and only about 18 percent of the anglophones are Catholic. Thus, for all intents and purposes, the discouragement of mixed marriages has meant the discouragement of marriages between those of the two language groups. In keeping with the recent ecumenical spirit, the official Church position discouraging such unions has softened; some villagers even state they would not object if their children chose to marry a Protestant Anglo-Canadian. This liberalism is probably more ideal than real, since many villagers are unlikely to be tested by such cases in the near future.

In spite of the societal changes which have somewhat weakened the forceful discouragement of marriages between Catholics and non-Catholics, it is still highly important for villagers' marital partners to be Catholic. The roles that villagers play in establishing and reinforcing relationships with kinsmen are often religiously based. Until recently, ritual kin positions could not be assumed by non-Catholics, and, if a villager married a non-Catholic, important roles, based in kin obligations and associated with life crises celebrations, would not have been open to the non-Catholic spouse.

Some villagers believe that Anglo-Canadian Protestants do not want as many children as Catholics do, and, hence, in a mixed marriage the happiness of the Catholic is thought to be at stake. Although marriages between Catholics and non-Catholics are permitted today, older beliefs remain that marriage to a non-Catholic will eventually lead to conflict over basic questions of how many children the couple will have and how the children will be educated.

In the Shippegan area, the largest group of Anglo-Canadians resides on Miscou Island. Opportunities for youngsters of Lameque Island to meet Anglo-Canadians of Miscou are rare; Miscou children attend elementary school on Miscou Island and Anglo-Canadian high schoolers board elsewhere in the province where they can attend English-language schools. More importantly, Miscou Island and its residents are deprecated by other residents of the area; Miscou is termed "the end of the earth." Only a few villagers ever go to Miscou, to hunt geese or to pick wild blueberries and cranberries. Various stories are related to discourage individuals from going to Miscou at all, e.g., "hunters get their car tires slashed"; "the people are rough there"; "the ferry won't be able to bring you back to Lameque and there would be no where to go on Miscou if you were stranded there." Residents of Ste. Marie appear to have little inclination or opportunity for meeting Miscou's Anglo-Canadians. As far as I know, there have never been any marriages between Anglo-Canadians of Miscou and villagers of Ste. Marie.

Some explanations can be suggested for the negative feelings that villagers hold towards Miscou's Anglo-Canadians. Firstly, people of Miscou, both francophone and anglophone, appear to be some of the poorest people in the area. Villagers of Ste. Marie ridicule those who are poor due to a lack of initiative, and poor English-speaking people may be marked for special deprecation. Secondly, as Miscou's Anglo-Canadians are the largest contingent of non-Acadians in the Shippegan area, they may be deprecated for only that reason. In the past, Acadians have been explicitly encouraged by priests to have little contact with Anglo-Canadians. Thus, the stories about Miscou may represent villagers' rationalization for avoidance behavior established decades ago. Or, the descriptions of Miscou may have a basis in fact; for example, hunters from beyond Miscou may get their car tires slashed there just as fishermen from beyond Lameque Island may have their traps destroyed if they attempt to fish in island waters to which they are not customarily admitted.

Those villagers who seek wage labor beyond the area usually go to Windsor-Detroit, Toronto, and New England, where English is soon learned. In these urban areas, individuals from the village have met and married anglophones. However, as mentioned above, non-Catholic anglophones are prohibited from taking part in interaction important to villagers. Participation in religious events--as godparent, confirmation sponsor, marriage witness, one who serves or assists the priest at the nuptial Mass--is also participation in kin-based events; responsibilities to one's kinsmen are often performed in a religious context. Marriage to a non-Catholic can be viewed as marriage to a partial person, for the non-Catholic is unable to play important roles in villagers' lives. However, the most commonly expressed regret that villagers voice about mixed marriages of kinsmen is that they are unable to communicate with the English-speaking spouses and children of the unions, for usually in such marriages English is the language used. Stories are told of anglophone spouses who are brought to the village to pass a vacation and who have spent the whole time in the house of their in-laws without being able to say so much as <u>bonjour</u>. Non-Catholic anglophone kinsmen living elsewhere--in Toronto, Detroit, or wherever--are usually in Ste. Marie only infrequently and for brief periods. Thus, in these brief visits their inability to play kin- and religiously-based roles is perhaps not as conspicuous as their inability to communicate with kin.

Villagers who work elsewhere in English North America and who marry anglophones do not return to the village to live. Living in a rural, economically depressed region, where social and economic opportunities are limited, might not appeal to many outsiders, no matter if there was ease or difficulty in speaking the local language. No doubt, though, most English monolingual spouses would probably not be eager to live in Ste. Marie where so few of the population are bilingual.

Language and religion are integral components in Acadian identity; differences in language and religion reflect differences in ethnic identity. In the above discussion I have stressed that Anglo-Canadians are not desired as mates because of language and religious differences, not because of differences in ethnic identity per se which is, however, implicitly involved as well.

The sense of Acadian peoplehood (stemming from the recognition of descent from the eighteenth century Acadians) appears to be most relevant for villagers in distinguishing themselves from those who are also French-speaking and Catholic, namely Quebeckers. Thus different aspects of Acadian identity are important in relation to different ethnic groups considered.

Opportunities for villagers to meet Quebeckers are limited, although some Quebeckers regularly vacation in the Shippegan area. As mentioned earlier, Acadians see themselves as being different from Quebeckers; for example, villagers report that Quebeckers are arrogant and snobbish and not as friendly and easy-going as Acadians. Thus, negative attitudes toward, and limited opportunities to meet, Quebeckers, probably account for the fact that only one villager's spouse is from Quebec.

In sum, local and ethnic origins are cultural factors which influence villagers' choices of mates. Villagers continue to marry Acadians from the island and especially from their own ecclesiastical parish (60 percent of the village marriages involve individuals from this parish); moreover, they tend to marry persons with whom they are already related (29 percent of the marriages--19 out of 66--are between people who were previously related.)[1] Those who marry outsiders live outside. In short, a new generation of villagers, descended from islanders for the most part, insure linguistic and cultural continuity in Ste. Marie.

As described above, then, isolation and lack of opportunity to meet Anglo-Canadians are important factors inhibiting the formation of mixed marriages in Ste. Marie. There are also characteristics within village life which directly or indirectly discourage marriage to Anglo-Canadians, or residence in the village if such a marriage takes place. Important responsibilities and interaction take place in a religious context; marriage to a local Acadian, French-speaking and Catholic, contributes to the possibility of one's maintaining smooth relationships with kin and villagers as a whole. Thus, although sharing the same physical environment, Anglo-Canadians and Acadians in the Shippegan area live in different social worlds. Speaking different languages, accepting different faiths, and having different frames of reference, the two ethnic groups coexist but live in worlds that seldom coincide.

Chapters Five and Six discussed the processes which minimize Anglo-Canadian contacts with villagers and which exclude entrance of Anglo-Canadians into village life. The next two chapters carry this theme further by considering some of the territorially delimited groups in which villagers participate and the kinds of interactions structured by these groups.

STRUCTURING INTERACTION: WITHIN THE PARISH

Villagers of Ste. Marie are part of social groupings within various activity, or social, fields. As participants in the fishery, they are part of an occupational (or industrial) field of worldwide proportions; markets, methods, capital investment, and the future of the fishery itself are governed by factors far removed from the village. Also, villagers of Ste. Marie are members of territorially delimited social groupings; household, neighborhood, village, and parish are but a few of the territorial units in which villagers interact.[1] This chapter discusses the processes by which villagers are incorporated into life essentially Acadian, how villagers are brought into interaction with others like themselves--French-speaking and Catholic.

THE HOUSEHOLD AND NEIGHBORHOOD

The household is a residence group comprising kinsmen and to some extent it has been discussed in the previous chapter. The nature of the neighborhood, too, is that of a kin-based enclave. Not all people in one neighborhood are related, but the members of one household usually have kinsmen in several other households in the neighborhood. As noted earlier, the close proximity of kinsmen's households is a matter of choice as well as chance. Some villagers have purchased property close to their kinsmen; other kinsmen have been given property by a common relative, and, hence, find themselves living adjacent to each other. The proximity of kin generally increases contacts between them. Individuals seek their neighboring kinsmen when it is necessary to borrow items, request a baby-sitter or transportation, or if a card game is being formed or impromptu visiting done. Daily face-to-face contacts, especially for women and children, are generally confined to the neighborhood and much of this activity within a neighborhood is thus between kin.

In years past neighbors cooperatively performed "jobs" such as cutting wood or carding wool, but today there are few opportunities for working together. Neighborhood dances and suppers, commonly held in conjunction with "jobs," are activities of the past. Neighborhood-based study groups associated with the cooperative movement in its formative years no longer exist. Sometimes an individual chooses to build, rather than to buy, a house, at which time some neighbors may assist in the work. Nevertheless, today formally organized activities involving largely neighborhood residents do not exist.

The relative importance of the neighborhood, village, and parish has changed in recent decades. The village has weakened in importance as a unit of interaction, while the neighborhood and parish have remained the same or increased in importance. That is, the locus of parish affairs, the church, has expanded its sponsorship of activities; the building of the community center and the establishment of regular events, such as dances and soirées, have enlarged the importance of the church and the church committees. Several secular groups, such as the Chambre de Commerce and the credit union, were recently formed by members of the parish. Hence, although the parish church has always been important in drawing parishioners together at weekly and seasonal religious events, the parish unit has recently increased in importance with regard to secular affairs. Furthermore, although the nature of the neighborhood has changed, informal interaction within the neighborhood has continued to be intense; today, however, interaction is largely between kinsmen of the neighborhood, rather than between non-kinsmen cooperating in economic activities.

THE VILLAGE

The village of Ste. Marie, as a territorial and social unit, is much like a <u>rang</u>, one division within ecclesiastical parishes of rural Quebec. As described by Fortin, the <u>rang</u> of the agricultural parish of Ste. Julienne, some forty years ago, was "the social unit of the community." Fortin wrote:

> It was in the "rang" that people gathered to share work in the "corvées" and to hold traditional "veillées," and was there also that the daily intercourse between the families took place. In fact, the "rang" was more or less cut off from the village [the church and service center] owing to the state of the roads. And covering the three or four miles which separated it from the village was considered quite a trip. The "rang" therefore constituted a rather isolated social unit for which the village played the role of the outside world. For the majority of the women and children, the weekly trip to the church or to the store was their only contact with the world at large (1968:92).

This description also seems to be applicable to the Ste. Marie of several decades ago. Ste. Marie was a unit socially independent from the parish; in fact, the village existed prior to St. Raphael Parish, which was not formed until 1937. In the 1940s, the parish cooperative grocery store was established near the church, but, not long after, a parish cooperative fish processing plant was established in Ste. Marie, and, thus, made Ste. Marie the focus of much, albeit seasonal, activity. As mentioned above, it is only in recent years that parish services, centralized near the church, have expanded, and the importance of village services diminished.

Stores are now found within the neighborhoods and, thus, villagers do not depend on one village store; increased mobility allows individuals to go beyond the village for various other services and facilities. Thus, today informal interaction is extremely limited between villagers who live in different neighborhoods of Ste. Marie.

Organized formal activity between villagers is similarly limited. Villagers elect representatives to the parish committee and, on special occasions, choose individuals to represent Ste. Marie (for example, the village princess at the parish Winter Carnival). Some sports competitions involve formation of village teams (for example, the women's broom-ball team which competes during Winter Carnival and the boys' softball and hockey teams).

The village, however, is not an administrative unit. There are no meetings to which all villagers are specifically invited; villagers are not responsible for fulfilling basic jobs or participating in certain activities as villagers.

Nevertheless, individuals have responsibilities to act in an acceptable way in interaction with neighbors and villagers. Traits generally considered desirable in relationships can be characterized as "egalitarianism" and "restraint." In an ideal sense, these characteristics imply a recognition that people have equal worth and that they are entitled to public respect and privacy. Egalitarianism and restraint are ideally characteristic of interpersonal relationships; however, in actual fact, villagers hold varying amounts of respect for each other according to such criteria as whether the individual is hard-working, cares for his family, is clever or "smart," and is generous to his friends. Villagers recognize differences in individual behavior and measure out their regard accordingly. Each villager also knows much about his neighbors' affairs. Here, as in Cat Harbour (Faris 1966), children are the eyes and ears of the community; there is little they do not learn and report to their parents concerning which fisherman caught three hundred pounds of lobster, which woman bought a new washing machine, where a car accident occurred, who was injured, and who was to blame, and so forth. A villager may express ignorance regarding an event of which he has full knowledge; this expression respects and protects a fellow villager's privacy. In the section below I discuss some aspects of these characteristics of interpersonal relationships, and I begin by discussing the characteristic of restraint.

A certain restraint typifies interaction of neighbors and villagers. When strangers are involved, this restraint becomes intensified and is more accurately described as suspicion. In former times, few strangers entered the area and those who did were often government officials. The Acadian experience, before and after the grand dérangement, indicated that strangers, especially those connected with the government, were not to be trusted. With increased government presence in the area (for example, Department of Fisheries Officers attempting to stop illegal fishing), strangers are often suspected to be government spies. I was naturally ascribed this role and undoubtedly there remain some villagers in Ste. Marie who believe my true identity as a government agent will ultimately be revealed.

The essence of the stranger is simply that the behavior of such an individual is unpredictable. Anyone who is not known is a stranger; anyone known in only one context could be a stranger as far as other contexts are concerned. The creation of an unusual situation never encountered before by two neighbors (e.g., a question regarding a household property boundary) may put them in the position of not being able to predict the others' behavior; that is, each is a stranger to the other in that particular situation. Hence, identifying strangers is a relative matter for villagers with membership in a general class of strangers being temporary and fluid according to the situation encountered.

Generally, however, the strangers who are most feared or viewed suspiciously are individuals who are not personally known in any context. Hence, the entrance of outsiders to Ste. Marie is not encouraged by villagers. Owners of tourist facilities are put in the awkward position of wanting to make a profit, yet not wanting to introduce strangers to the community who might be troublesome. Such facilities are not publicly advertised, but they are privately advertised by word of mouth; customers usually come through the recommendation of relatives or long time customers. Undoubtedly there would be more customers if owners were willing to accept strangers into their midst; instead less money is made to insure that a minimum of strangers enter the village even on a temporary basis.

When an individual gets into some difficulty with the government, (perhaps in regard to payment of taxes or the reporting of income) this difficulty is attributed not to chance but to the interference by some stranger, or enemy, of the individual. Difficulty with legal or governmental authorities is considered to stem from someone's intervention rather than from a random or systematic check on the part of government officers.

Because interaction among villagers is described as restrained does not mean that relations are strained. Generally speaking, villagers are friendly, warm, and generous with each other and show affection and concern for their fellows. Nevertheless, as described by one oldster, contact between villagers is not carried on the way it was in earlier days. Before, when there were not so many relatives living in proximate households, both social and economic contacts with neighbors and villagers were extensive. Today interaction is largely conducted between kinsmen living close by, and there may be relatively few opportunities or excuses to have contacts of any depth with unrelated neighbors. Hence, in some cases neighbors may enjoy a cordial and friendly relationship similar to that between kinsmen. In other cases, though, neighbors may barely know each other and thus find it necessary to treat each other respectfully and, in some contexts, even suspiciously as strangers.

I have also described villagers' relationships as being characterized by egalitarianism; villagers describe themselves as being equal, with no villager being "better" than another. By so doing, however, they ignore their socioeconomic differences, which in some contexts, make certain villagers better-off in income and prestige than others.

Although substantial socioeconomic differences between villagers are of recent origin, some differences have probably existed as long as has the village. In the mid-nineteenth century Perley wrote that island fishermen who owned their own fishing gear and boats, and who processed fish prior to sale, received a greater return for their catch than those who sold fish only partially processed and who were forced to rent boats and gear (Perley 1852). By the end of the nineteenth century and beginning of the twentieth, several village men owned and operated small lobster canning shops which employed women and youngsters to cook, clean, and pack lobster for resale elsewhere. It is difficult to assess if the capital investment of these villagers fifty years ago actually resulted in substantially more income than their fellows. Today villagers describe life as always having been hard and no villager or village family ever having had much money.

Nevertheless, the histories of some village families indicate that socioeconomic differences have existed for at least several decades. Some families have several children who have been educated beyond the high school level; others have none. Some older houses (forty to sixty years old) are larger and apparently better constructed than others. Some of the older men in the village consistently held leadership positions within the area, as members of the fabrique (a church committee), as members of the local school board, or as organizers in the co-op movement. Constellations of features cluster with certain families or individuals and indicate that there were differences in villagers in terms of leadership abilities and interests, in ambitions for themselves and their children, and in economic well-being.

Individuals having certain specialized occupations undoubtedly had more importance. Such people included teachers, as educated and literate people, storekeepers, as individuals able to extend credit, and the blacksmith, as someone possessing a skill necessary to village life. However, until quite recently teachers were notoriously low paid and there is no evidence that village storekeepers or blacksmiths of past years ever became particularly well-off.

Priests and nuns (the latter have been resident in the parish since 1949 and have primarily served as school teachers) held the highest positions of power and prestige in the parish. As individuals who were not originally of the parish held the highest positions in the parish, egalitarianism could be maintained. That is, there was no competition for the highest status in the parish (parish priest); this was a position to which parishioners could not aspire. The position was appointed and, for the most part, the giving and accepting of the appointment had little, if anything, to do with the will of parishioners. Thus the traditional rural parish power structure encouraged egalitarianism among laymen, as they all had little power and prestige in comparison to that of the parish elite, the priests and nuns.

Today the priest's leadership in secular affairs has diminished somewhat. Positions of parish leadership are usually assumed by the better-educated and financially better-off members of the village (teachers, captains of offshore fishing vessels, businessmen, and the wives of such men). However, the existence of only a few leadership positions, none of which constitutes a status of officially elected representative (such as a mayor) helps to maintain a semblance of political equality in the village; no one has authority to tell anyone else what to do.

WITHIN THE PARISH 133

Although in earlier times, there may have been only modest variation in wealth, power, and prestige, this is not so today. Household incomes in Ste. Marie range from a few thousand dollars to $15,000 - $20,000 and the number of household members supported by such incomes varies considerably. A few households composed of no more than five or six members enjoy incomes of $15,000 or more, while other households of eight to ten may be supported on a yearly income of $3,000 to $4,000. As a result, there are wide differences among households in material goods and standards of living.

Households in which income is ample and members few contain modern appliances (electric stoves, refrigerators, deep freezers, clothes washers and dryers, dishwashers and color televisions), new cars, and snowmobiles (costing between $500 and $1,000). A few low income households do not have running water and the only major appliances are a refrigerator and television. Most village households fall somewhere between these two extremes and enjoy conveniences of running water, central heating, and major appliances.

Though resentment or jealousy may be felt and expressed by poorer villagers toward wealthier ones, the strongest comments about the amount of money an individual has and what he does with it are usually reserved for individuals who make their money in the village and from villagers. These individuals, such as storekeepers and brokers handling the fish catch, may be criticized for being "too ambitious" in entering into various projects or "too tight" financially in attempting to make as much money as possible. This group of people is circumspect in spending money for clothes or new cars and luxury items; the wife of one storekeeper expressed considerable hesitation and embarrassment about wearing a new dress to church as she was afraid people would think her "stuck up" or snobbish in having something new and better than that of others. In fact, in going to church most people are fairly consistent in wearing the same "good" clothing. Those who make money from village businesses are eager to volunteer to anyone information on the costs of their enterprises, e.g., the taxes paid, the amounts expended for property improvement and for supplies or equipment; according to their descriptions it would appear that profits are slight to nonexistent.

Theoretically every man's house is open to all villagers and all are on equal terms. In actual fact, however, if villagers are unrelated, do not live in the same neighborhood, or have quite different income levels, contact is minimal; there are many houses into which members of other households have never entered and probably will never enter. In recreation or leisure time entertainment, interaction is similarly restricted.

Although there is socioeconomic differentiation among villagers, the village population cannot be termed stratified or class-structured. The village does not contain enough of a variety of status positions or a large enough population to identify groups of people or statuses which differ significantly in "power, wealth, and prestige" (Morris 1968:168). It is possible, of course, to rank villagers according to the amount of personal wealth and power they possess, but this ranking would be relatively continuous and only a few villagers would rank at either extreme. Kin ties are more powerful than ties of wealth or power and, hence, interaction takes place largely within kin groupings, rather than among persons of the same socioeconomic level.

In sum, despite some economic, educational, and social differentiation within the village, villagers share interests and participate in many of the same activities: they shop in the same stores (though some may have more money to spend than others), they send their children to the same schools (though some children have more of a chance of being sent to college than others), they sit together in the same church where they must abide by the same obligations, and they worry about the same problems--over-fishing by outsiders, the low price for fish, the small size of catches. Although some villagers are more important in parish activities and more successful in monetary affairs, these individuals usually project the image that they are like all others and that all villagers are equal.

THE PARISH

The parish is the smallest unit of organization within the Catholic Church; all Catholics who reside in the territory demarcated as St. Raphael Parish are members of the parish church. St. Raphael Parish also represents a minimum local unit of administration and organization in secular affairs.

Before considering interaction on a parish level, a few salient features of the parish can be recapitulated. First, St. Raphael Parish includes the villages of Ste. Marie-sur-Mer, St. Raphael-sur-Mer, Cap Bateau, and Haut St. Raphael; the first three villages extend along much of the eastern shore of Shippegan Island; Haut St.

Raphael lies inland. The four villages are much alike in settlement pattern and sociocultural features.

St. Raphael-sur-Mer now represents a center for certain parish activities. Various facilities in that village belong to the parish as a whole: the church, the priest's residence, the nuns' residence, the elementary school, the community center, the cooperative grocery store, and the credit union.

Balancing off the importance of these facilities in St. Raphael are the wharf in Ste. Marie, and, until a few years ago, the large usine in Cap Bateau. The latter establishment is now closed. Until recent years, then, the villages of Cap Bateau, St. Raphael, and Ste. Marie each contained facilities of importance to the parish as a whole.

The Parish: A Religious Field

Those parts of St. Raphael Parish which can be physically seen and most easily described are the land, buildings, and property located at the center of St. Raphael village. Here stand the large white church, built some sixty years ago, and the residences of the parish priest and nuns. Beyond the priest's house is the parish cemetery, with its neat rows of white wooden crosses and gravestones. There are no family plots; instead graves are laid out in chronological order. Further west of the cemetery is a large open field used by parishioners in sports activities. A few hundred yards east of the church is the community center.

The nuns' residence is seldom entered by parishioners; the priest's residence is usually visited only in time of trouble or unusual circumstances, e.g., in arranging for a marriage ceremony.

The cemetery is entered only at funerals or times of remembrance when flowers are placed on the graves of deceased parishioners.

The sports field is largely frequented by youngsters and young men who play softball in summer and hockey in winter. The community center is a familiar place for many parishioners, depending on their individual interests. If the parishioner enjoys dances, bingo, and card games, he may often be at the center when such affairs are held; if he is not interested in these activities, he may seldom enter the center.

The church, however, is the physical nucleus to which all parishioners, regardless of sex, age, or special interests, are drawn to attend weekly Mass. At Mass villagers are given an opportunity to demonstrate and reaffirm their membership in the Catholic Church as a whole and in St. Raphael Parish in particular; this opportunity also exists at special celebrations of the liturgical year, such as Christmas and Easter, and at ceremonies connected with life crises of parishioners.

It is both the duty and right of parishioners to celebrate their own and others' life crises and to take part in the weekly and yearly religious activities of the church. Villagers are generally active Catholics and orient their lives through sacraments which celebrate life crises, attend Mass weekly, and structure their lives by the passing liturgical seasons. In Ste. Marie, at the time of fieldwork, there were no conjugal units which had not been married in the Church; there were no babies over the age of three months who had not been baptized; and most villagers, with the exception of some teenagers and unmarried young adults, appeared to attend Mass regularly.

Baptism is the single sacramental celebration which is usually attended only by the immediate family. Recently, however, some baptisms in the parish have taken place at weekend Masses, thus directly involving all parishioners. First Communion and Confirmation ceremonies represent the child's achieving more mature and responsible religious statuses, and take place in front of all parishioners, or at least all those who can find place in the church; large groups of children receive their First Communion or are confirmed at the same time and hence large numbers of relatives and neighbors usually attend these events. The Mass celebration of marriages, the ordination of a parish boy into the priesthood, or the entrance of a parish girl into a religious order, are open to all parishioners. Funerals within the parish receive varying amounts of attendants, the number depending on the circumstances. For example, the funeral of a young man accidentally killed was heavily attended, while the funeral of an aged parishioner who had been living in the Shippegan old people's home received less attendance.

Villagers are expected to attend Mass weekly, either on Saturday night or Sunday morning. Attendance at Mass provides an opportunity to see other parishioners and to receive parish news in announcements made by the priest, but it does not represent an occasion for intensive interaction among parishioners. Casual greetings are exchanged between women prior to or after Mass, but long conversations are absent. Some men converse outside the church until the last possible moment before Mass begins, at which time they join their wives and children inside. In church, conversations are at a minimum and restlessness or noise on the part of all but the very youngest parishioners is not tolerated, either by the congregation or the priest.

Many villagers regularly go together to Mass in one car. The owner of a car which has extra room will transport the same people weekly; the car owner receives a small cash payment in return. The rides to and from Mass provide opportunities for the exchange of information regarding a wealth of topics--the week's activities (past and future), fishing, the weather, the condition of gardens, houses, clothing, hair styles, and health of those in the car, their relatives, and those individuals seen at church or on the way to and from the church.

The Parish: A Social Field

Parish-sponsored annual events may have little overt relation to religion, but such events provide occasions for parishioners to get together and demonstrate interest and pride in the church affairs. The Parish Committee sponsors weekly dances for teenagers, monthly soirées for adults, bi-annual bingo-raffles, weekly card games in the winter; another committee organizes sports activities for boys and young men. All but the sports activities are sources of revenue for the church. Special parish-sponsored events include a Mother's Day party and the Winter Carnival, a pre-Lenten weekend of activity involving games and contests, dances, and selection of a carnival queen. In short, there is a social event of some type planned or taking place at the community center all year round. Some of the events only appeal to one sex or to one age level, but the overall result is that members of many households are frequently engaged in some event planned by the parish church committees.

The Parish Committee is composed of two elected representatives from each of the four villages and the parish priest. As mentioned earlier, villagers who hold parish leadership positions are among the better educated and financially better-off. Women from Ste. Marie have often held positions representing the village on the committee; all of these women were wives of offshore fishermen and were better educated than many other villagers. One businessman and several school teachers from the village have also held positions on the committee.

Usually when someone has held a position for one term, he or she will be asked to hold it again. Many parishioners are not interested in holding office, and incumbents are commonly retained. Holding a committee position undoubtedly involves some prestige for the individual, but it is certainly not a major source of prestige for members from Ste. Marie, all of whom have achieved more than their fellows through marriage, education, or professional status. Their membership on the committee underlines their slightly higher position, but it is not the source of it.

The committee has considerable freedom in making decisions and in organizing parish activities. The priest has de facto veto power, but for the most part he is an advisor whose opinion is requested. However, the priest is responsible for handling and banking the rather large sums of money brought into the parish treasury. At the end of the year, both the committee and the priest give reports at an open parish meeting at which committee members for the new year are elected.

The Parish Priest

Recent reform in the Catholic Church in general has lessened the importance of the priest and increased the importance and participation of parishioners in administrative matters and in religious ritual. Prior to the formation of the Parish Committee in 1969, the priest had much more responsibility for the parish administration and parishioners were limited to serving on the fabrique, a committee which was to assist the priest in parish affairs; the members were appointed by the priest and apparently had little power.

Most parishioners are relatively sophisticated in their awareness of changes within the church. Some changes have been superficial. Women seldom wear head coverings at church and slacks are now not unusual female attire at Mass; folksongs, accompanied by a guitar-bass-drums ensemble, are normal fare at Mass in St. Raphael. Other changes have been more substantial. Villagers describe saints as having "lost their jobs" and parishioners have recently suggested having the statues of saints removed from the parish church. Laymen in the parish have increasingly important roles in taking part in religious celebrations, such as distributing Communion and giving readings at Mass; the priest and church hierarchy, though respected, are not considered infallible or necessarily even likeable. Topics such as whether priests should be allowed to marry and the merits of general, as opposed to individual, confession are debated by villagers.

In general, priests have made a conscious effort to diminish their roles as the leaders or authorities in parish affairs. Earlier responsibilities held by priests have been consequently absorbed by parish committees or individual leaders.

The position of the priest as the moral leader in the parish remains unquestioned. The priest is called upon to settle family quarrels and to give advice; he is looked upon as an authority on many subjects. The priest is the best-educated person in the parish and is one of its few fluent bilingual speakers. He has many potentially influential connections beyond the parish boundaries. Nevertheless, the reputation that priests hold and their relationship with parishioners vary, and are often functions of the priest's personality and demeanor. Because a man is a priest, he is entitled to a measure of respect from most people. However, by his actions rather than through his office, the priest must earn the affection and regard of his parishioners.

Because of specific conditions in St. Raphael in the last several years, few parishioners have had personal relationships with the resident priests. The priest at St. Raphael is also responsible for the mission church at Pigeon Hill, and, hence, has over three hundred households and about two thousand individuals to serve. Moreover, as of spring, 1972, there had been three different priests in the parish in as many years; this allowed little opportunity for these priests to know well the parishioners and their individual problems. At this point, the priest represents something of a symbol of the parish, much as do the buildings--the church and community center--rather than representing an individual who has influence on parishioners in personal terms and in face-to-face interaction.

As described in this chapter, villagers are incorporated into territorially-based fields: household, neighborhood, village, and parish. Within the household and neighborhood, interaction is essentially defined by kin role behavior; life-long obligations to a wide range of people are fulfilled in these contexts. Within the village, interaction among non-kinsmen is informal and characterized by egalitarianism and restraint. Interaction in the parish in religious and secular church affairs brings villagers together weekly and in a yearly cycle of liturgical seasons and formal events; individual life crises are shared by parishioners, each of whom experiences the same cycle of events and celebrates them before largely the same audience. Thus, in territorial fields villagers constantly interact with people who are of the same language, religion, and background. By such interaction, ties between these fellow Acadians are maintained and strengthened.

The next chapter describes interaction between villagers and those beyond the parish; characteristic of this interaction is the presence of intermediaries (organizational and individual) which lessen villagers' contacts with Anglo-Canadians.

STRUCTURING INTERACTION: THE PARISH AND BEYOND

The parish is both a field of religious activity and a unit of secular administration. Though the parish as a religious field is an organizational unit in the larger structure of the Catholic Church, for my interests the importance of the parish is not in its role as an articulating unit between the Church and the people (though admittedly it has such a role), but as an integrating unit which serves to bring parishioners together in certain kinds of social and religious activities.

As a secular administrative unit, however, the parish derives much of its importance through being an articulator between the government and the people. Parish associations benefit parishioners in parish-delimited activity, but they also serve importantly to aid parishioners in dealing with the government and problem situations beyond the parish.

In this chapter I discuss the role of parish organizations as intermediaries between parishioners, including villagers of Ste. Marie-sur-Mer, and the government; I also discuss the role of individuals who serve as intermediaries between villagers and representatives of the world beyond Lameque Island, a world which includes anglophones.

GOVERNING AND DEALING WITH THE GOVERNMENT

To understand the political or governmental fields in which villagers are represented, it is important to note that there is no local level form of elected government in the village or parish. Lameque is the only island settlement that has been incorporated as a village. In recent years, the topic of incorporation was discussed in St. Raphael Parish, but the idea was objected to by many local people who believed incorporation would only result in additional taxes for services they did not need, such as local fire and police protection and snow removal. Currently snow removal is a provincial responsibility; police protection comes from an RCMP detachment located on the mainland. A fire department in Lameque town will provide assistance, but equipment is old and the distance between Lameque and St. Raphael is such that if a fire starts in the parish the building is usually totally destroyed.

Though unincorporated, the parish and its organization represent an administrative unit akin to a municipality. Admittedly, there is no single official body running all activities of the parish. Church committees organize various religious and social activities; the Chambre de Commerce, cooperative store, and the credit union take care of the civic and financial well-being of the parish and its members. However, committee members or officers of various parish associations are often drawn from the same group of people. The overlapping membership of formal leaders creates a core of parishioners who have an active part in all parish activities, and whose widespread interests and influence are similar to those of a board of aldermen or councilors in a municipality.

The cooperative store and the credit union are associations which primarily benefit members who voluntarily choose to accept services and responsibilities with the groups. The Chambre de Commerce, however, is a group whose projects and responsibilities affect all parishioners whether or not they are members. Though less than thirty parishioners are members, the group plans projects which, if approved by parishioners, affect the whole parish. The Chambre de Commerce also serves as a body through which requests and criticisms are channelled to the government. In the past, parish political committees apparently served this function by contacting appropriate officeholders when particular needs were felt locally. Today this old function of political party committees has been largely assumed by the nonpartisan Chambre de Commerce.

Political committees today only meet when necessary, such as when representatives must be selected to serve at province-wide conventions. Only during election periods are committee members overtly involved in political activities; during an election campaign the committee organizes public meetings at which programs of the particular party are discussed. Less than fifty parishioners are actively involved in the committees for the two major political parties, the Liberals and the Conservatives. The New Democratic Party and the recently formed Parti Acadien receive little support in the parish. Villagers do not support candidates running as independents, or as members of minority parties, for they believe such individuals would be relatively powerless if elected; only if a minority government were in power would members of the smaller parties wield influence. Traditionally French speakers in New

Brunswick have supported the Liberal Party at both the provincial and federal levels of government.

Participation in parish associations is not obligatory for local people and few are inclined to participate. Similarly leadership positions need not be accepted. However, certain individuals are recognized as having continuing interests in the associations and are assumed to be willing to act as officers or committeemen. Hence, during the summer, meetings of the Chambre de Commerce are not held since important members are busy with seasonal fishing activities and cannot attend meetings. Once an individual has begun accepting leadership positions in the parish, he will be under regular pressure to continue holding these positions.

As individuals participating in the Chambre de Commerce have no mandate from the people to perform various functions, programs may or may not be publicly supported, depending on the situations involved. The installation of street lights throughout the parish had popular support and there was little objection to the project. However, when the Chambre de Commerce moved to erect a welcoming sign to St. Raphael Parish on the outskirts of Ste. Marie, some villagers objected as they feared the village's independent existence was being threatened. Consequently, when the Chambre de Commerce erected the welcome sign just outside of Ste. Marie, the village's largest grocery store promptly put up a sign on its storefront declaring the place as "Ste. Marie-sur-Mer."

Generally, the Chambre de Commerce avoids controversial projects and instead handles routine parish problems for which support is relatively assured. Controversial and special-interest problems are handled by temporarily formed committees. "Government by committee" has been noted to characterize social life in Bremmes (Barnes 1954:52), the Norwegian island parish which has been previously mentioned as having similarities with Ste. Marie and the larger parish. In St. Raphael Parish, the existence of two kinds of governing committees, those of standing or executive committees of enduring associations and those of temporary, special-interest committees, allows the segregation of the stable organization handling routine parish affairs from the potentially disruptive organizations concerned with controversial affairs. The long-standing committees of parish associations remain neutral and uninvolved in divisive issues, and thus are able to function with some measure of public acceptance. Controversial committees, such as the committee formed to further the interests of certain parishioners in the conflict over area medical personnel, can be rapidly formed and disbanded when problems are resolved or committee effectiveness has diminished; the committee's disappearance signals the end or the resolution of the conflict. Though interpersonal relationships may remain disrupted for some time, there will be no formal bodies through which disruption can be channelled or maintained.

Many contacts between villagers and the government are channelled through local groups or committees. Part of the administrative structure established for handling development programs in Northeastern New Brunswick involves the creation of regional citizens' groups which serve as intermediaries between local people and the government. Conseil Régional Area Nord-Est (C.R.A.N.) functions as a liason between people residing in Northeastern New Brunswick and governmental agencies planning programs of change (such as the Community Improvement Corporation). The official purpose of C.R.A.N. is to encourage local people to voice aspirations for their communities and to work with the government in implementing their own plans for improvement. C.R.A.N. is based in Bathurst and, though supporting various issues of interest to Shippegan people, it has not had as much importance for people of Shippegan as for those elsewhere, particularly those who live close to Bathurst.

Instead, local people continue to register their suggestions or criticisms of government policy through local bodies, such as the Chambre de Commerce and special action groups, or by direct expressions of displeasure. Special action groups or committees are formed on occasion according to need. While I was in the field, parishioners, along with others of the Shippegan-Caraquet area, vigorously protested the government's investigation of the sinking of two sister ships fishing herring from Lameque, the Lady Audette and Lady Dorianne. The mysterious sinkings took place within a period of six months and resulted in the loss of nine area fishermen, including four from Lameque Island, two of whom were from St. Raphael Parish, and one of these from Ste. Marie. Public meetings were called to consider the affair, much of which related to the future of a third sister ship, the Marc Guylaine; a committee was appointed to pursue the demands agreed upon at the meetings. Despite an absence of funds to support the committee's efforts, it was successful in having many of the demands met, including the eventual government condemning of the Marc Guylaine as being unsafe and the opening of a government inquest to consider more thoroughly various issues connected with the sinkings (see the Appendix for elaboration on the Marc Guylaine affair). Although such tragedies, and the resulting public actions, are not common, there have been similar cases in the past, e.g., the concerted effort by local fishermen to get government compensation for lobster traps damaged or destroyed in an unusually severe storm.

Some local people directly express their displeasure regarding political events, and often express it in a destructive way; for example, a politician backing unpopular policies may find his summer chalet mysteriously destroyed by fire. Recently, the large snowmobile (provided by the provincial government to afford transportation over the ice from Miscou to Lameque Island) was destroyed, reportedly by disgruntled residents of Miscou who had been demanding the construction of a bridge and were instead awarded a snowmobile.

Such destructive behavior must be viewed within the context of general mischief-making common in New Brunswick where favorite Halloween pranks are burning down buildings, usually old barns, abandoned houses, schools, or outbuildings. Nevertheless, the kinds of items and buildings destroyed, and their ownership, suggest that all such incidents cannot be regarded as neutral or nonpolitical acts. This type of destruction often appears to be the expression of displeasure by persons frustrated with normal channels of communication and redress and perhaps this frustration is due to the weakness of local-level political and governing structure.

Government representatives in the area (e.g., tax assessors and fish and game wardens) are usually bilingual and thus villagers are able to communicate with them. At the County Court House in Bathurst, villagers are also able to receive services in French.

Despite the growing emphasis on providing bilingual services, a surprising number of government documents are supplied in English in the French-speaking areas of the province. These documents often involve relatively unimportant subjects; for example, certain signs and pamphlets at the Shippegan town government-run liquor store and a voter registration list for Ste. Marie are in English. Other instances of English usage involve more serious matters. For example, English monolingual census takers were appointed in French-speaking areas in the 1971 census; English monolingual members of the R.C.M.P. have been stationed in a predominantly French-speaking area of New Brunswick. Such questionable actions on the part of the government serve as regular reminders that English is still the "first" and official language of the province.

THE BILINGUAL: INTERMEDIARY BETWEEN VILLAGERS AND GOVERNMENT

In light of the emphasis government places on English, it is not strange that many villagers believe English is the important language to use in getting anything done with the provincial or federal government. When contact with the government is necessary, family members who speak or write English are often called upon for assistance; it is assumed that this is the most efficient way of dealing with the government.

The role of the bilingual person who serves as an intermediary between villagers and government is repeated in villagers' dealings with government through the parish associations and committees. Although bilingualism does not insure that an individual will be selected for formal leadership positions, leaders are characteristically bilingual. Being bilingual indicates that the person has received more education and/or experience in areas beyond the island than most others, and these characteristics are considered to be advantageous in performing leadership roles. Bilingualism is not just a fortuitous skill held by leaders, but is locally considered an important, if not necessary, prerequisite for leadership.

Village or parish leaders will often be placed in positions where bilingualism is important. For example, individuals who attend province wide conventions of the Liberal and Conservative parties find themselves in contexts where English is the working language and English monolinguals are the important leaders of both parties. There are, of course, federal and provincial politicians who are bilingual. Acadians represent the Shippegan area at the provincial and federal levels of government; also Acadians have held various important high-level government positions and in the 1960s the Premier of New Brunswick was an Acadian. Generally, however, most bilingual politicians in New Brunswick are native French speakers. A few English-speaking provincial politicians have been learning French, which is locally interpreted to mean they have aspirations for higher office. Nevertheless, even provincial cabinet-level politicians can remain monolingual English and unabashedly use English in contexts in which it is highly inappropriate. For example, at the Shippegan Fisheries Festival in 1971, the Provincial Minister of Fisheries gave a speech in English to a crowd of local people; according to the 1971 census only about 15 percent of the population in Shippegan Civil parish is bilingual (Statistics Canada 1973). The crowd politely received the speech, but there was considerable restlessness on its part; probably few in the crowd understood anything of what was said.

Acadian patriotic groups, such as the Société des Acadiens du Nouveau-Brunswick, have begun demanding sub-departments for provincial education, one dealing with the education of francophones and the other dealing with the education of anglophones; they are asking for one Minister of Education over the two branches, and for two sub-ministers. For many Acadians it seems apparent that if Anglo-Canadians are included in any societal fields, such as provincial government and the civil service, Acadians are always the bilinguals who must speak English to the monolingual Anglo-Canadians. Thus setting up separate education departments has been suggested as an alternative, in which francophones and anglophones would get "separate, but equal" treatment in their own languages and by their own people.

In effect, this is what French-speaking Catholics struggled for at the turn of the century when they attained separate French parishes; in these parishes French became the working language in all church affairs and Acadian bishops were appointed to dioceses in which francophones lived. Previously English-speaking Irish priests and bishops had controlled the parishes and hierarchy of the Catholic Church in New Brunswick; it was only after several decades of disruption and controversy that Acadians gained French-speaking priests, parishes, and bishops (Thorburn 1961:24-31 passim).

During approximately the same period, there was also conflict between French and English over language use in schools. In French areas such as Shippegan, there was eventually de facto approval of French as the language of instruction; however, little assistance was given by the government to further the French language in education; supplies of materials and books were usually in English.[1]

With the more recent involvement of the government in education and other affairs it had previously largely ignored, and with the increasing militancy of Acadians to protect their customary rights, questions of governmental authority and language use will become increasingly important. In the provincial government, only three of the fourteen departments have "an ethnic origin distribution reasonably proportional to the ethnic origin distribution of the population of the province." Additionally, only in the Department of Fisheries could French be used at all levels (Thorburn 1971: 27-29). To be sure, government policies favoring bilingualism in the civil service should increasingly bring bilingual people into positions at various levels of authority in all provincial departments. Yet, until bilingualism becomes prevalent enough in the government and civil service for villagers to recognize its existence and to demand bilingual contacts, the need will continue for local-level leaders to be bilingual.

In the meantime, then, bilingualism continues to be characteristic of villagers who hold positions of responsibility in parish committees and associations. Bilingualism is locally regarded as a valuable skill and as an essential characteristic of leaders who deal with Anglo-dominated governmental or political bodies. These bilingual leaders serve as intermediaries between French-speaking villagers and English-speaking individuals, or groups, who participate in the same activity fields.

ON BEING FRANCOPHONE IN AN ANGLOPHONE WORLD

When villagers leave the Shippegan area, it takes very little time for them to travel into an essentially anglophone world. Though certain important features, such as highway signs, normally will continue to be written in both French and English, it will not take many hours of driving until the R.C.M.P. representatives policing that highway will be found to be English monolinguals; at roadside restaurants the menus will be written in English and the waitresses will speak only English. Nor does one have to go far from Shippegan to find similar difficulties in other transportation areas; signs and announcements in regional airports and train stations are commonly provided in English only.

Problems relating to transportation are only one area in which francophone monolinguals can experience difficulties. For many, however, this represents no difficulty for they seldom travel or, if they do, they confine themselves to relatively "safe" destinations and use relatively "safe" means of transportation. Casual vacationing takes place in Quebec where French language services are assured. Areas in which English is usually spoken, e.g., Toronto, Halifax, are visited only if kin or francophone friends live there, people on whom one can depend to smooth the way.

"Safe" means of transportation sometimes take the form of private taxis; almost any person with a car in good condition is a potential taxi driver, though some individuals do provide such services on a regular basis. If someone in Ste. Marie needs to go to Moncton for a doctor's appointment or to Edmundston to inquire about a job, a quick, comfortable means is by taxi. In part, the popularity of taxis can be explained by the lack of good public transportation in the area and the convenience that taxis afford. However, reliance on private taxis with bilingual drivers is but another strategem employed by monolingual villagers to cope with an anglophone world. Bilingual drivers insure, for example, that in stops during the trip, the villager will not be embarrassed or made uncomfortable by his inability to speak English; in emergencies the bilingual driver may be able to resolve difficulties with which the francophone monolingual cannot cope.

Many villagers have experienced embarrassment, discomfort, and sometimes real hardship when thrust into the anglophone world. Villagers who were students at the province's English language Teacher's College were forced to learn English quickly and well so that their studies could continue. Others have gone into English-speaking regions of the province to seek work, and, finding work with a construction crew or at a factory, have been forced by necessity to learn English. Such experiences, though hard and perhaps resulting in bitter memories, resulted from choices made by the individuals involved. Similar trying experiences undergone by villagers were not chosen, and these experiences have created particularly bitter memories. When someone is seriously ill, he or she will commonly be transferred to a hospital outside of northeastern New Brunswick. These hospitals, such as the one at St. John, are often in areas where English is commonly spoken and

English is the language of hospital employees--doctors, nurses, and aides. Villagers tell harrowing stories of their being ill and alone for days or weeks in a hospital where it was impossible to understand what was being done to them, why, and with what predicted results. For those who remain in hospitals for some time, it may not be possible to have the luxury of a bilingual intermediary between themselves and the monolingual hospital staff. Some francophone service groups located in anglophone areas attempt to fill these hospital, and similar, needs; however, sometimes the needs are not filled, as villagers from Ste. Marie will attest.

This chapter has discussed the villagers' and parishioners' dealings with individuals and political or governmental bodies based beyond the island. Such dealings often involve contacts with monolingual English speakers. However, villagers can avoid interactions with these monolingual anglophones by utilizing bilingual individuals and organizations which serve as intermediaries. Hence, villagers do not need to be bilingual to handle their political affairs. Informal contacts between villagers and the English-speaking world may also be buffered by intermediaries. In a number of contexts, however, insulating of contacts is not possible, and monolingual francophones may experience, sometimes in disconcerting ways, their minority status within New Brunswick and Canada as a whole.

ETHNIC PERSISTENCE, ETHNICITY, AND CONFLICT

The purpose of this study has been to account for the ethnic persistence of Acadians in Ste. Marie-sur-Mer, a rural fishing village in northeastern New Brunswick, Canada. In this chapter I summarize my findings and present suggestions for the further study of ethnic persistence, ethnicity, and ethnic conflict.

ETHNIC PERSISTENCE IN STE. MARIE

In this study the retention and use of the French language were used as indicators of the ethnic persistence of residents of Ste. Marie. In northeastern New Brunswick, French language retention is high among those of French origin. Vallee has suggested that ethnic persistence of the Acadian population is largely a result of social structural factors; persistence is possible because of "institutional completeness," or "community closure," in which a full complement of institutions are available to serve the Acadians. A structurally plural society makes possible the retention of cultural and linguistic differences (Vallee 1969; 1971).

In earlier chapters, I suggested that Vallee's approach obscures the nature of society in northeastern New Brunswick; I questioned if a range of institutions exists to fill the needs of the French-speakers, and if the existing institutions have relevance to the francophone population at large. English-speaking Canadians comprise 37 percent of northern and eastern New Brunswick and I suggested that the concept of community closure contributed little to understanding the ongoing relations between the area's English- and French-speakers.

Instead I proposed to follow an approach of Fredrik Barth in accounting for ethnic group persistence. Thus, I examined the structure of contacts between villagers and Anglo-Canadians in order to discover the cultural factors which incorporate, or bring together, local Acadians, and exclude non-Acadians from the village and parish context. I attempted to discover how ongoing interaction is structured so that contacts with Anglo-Canadians are minimized and contacts with fellow Acadians are intensified in frequency and importance.

I first examined economic and domestic realms of local life and found patterns of exclusion in religious, residential, and kinship-based activities in Ste. Marie. In the discussion of economic activities, I noted that hiring is done through kin and acquaintance channels and by such recruitment village fishermen, for example, are seldom put in contact with English-speaking crew members, though both inshore and offshore vessels in which anglophones fish are based in the area. Furthermore a variety of economic networks in which village men once participated, and which sometimes included anglophones, has shrunk with the villagers' changing patterns of economic adaptation. Unlike Acadians living in other areas of the Maritime Provinces, Ste. Marie men concentrate their work activities within the village or island context and do not find it necessary to migrate for employment. In essence, economic change, including the relative prosperity of recent years, has not exposed villagers to increased contacts with Anglo-Canadians, nor brought about acculturation.

The inner domestic core of villagers' lives is kept free from the influence of strangers, and particularly the influence of anglophones; spouses are selected from among francophones of the island, parish, or village itself, and frequently these spouses are from a corpus of people with whom some kind of kin tie can already be claimed. Though individuals who had once been members of the village had married strangers, anglophones and/or non-Catholics, they have established residence outside the village. As a result, villagers are francophone, Catholic, and of local origins. Such characteristics of villagers have obvious relevance in influencing enculturation and acquisition of ethnic identity and language skills by children.

I next described the territorial fields in which villagers participate and the ways in which interaction is channelled locally. Villagers participate in, and are incorporated into, local life through membership and activities as Catholics and parishioners, neighbors and villagers, kinsmen or householders. Religion, kin ties, residence, and language are features which indicate potential membership in Ste. Marie and St. Raphael Parish; proper performance in relation to these features is essential in validating that membership.

Much of the villagers' activities takes place within relatively close proximity to Ste. Marie-sur-Mer, and a certain local life exists independent of transactions and affairs elsewhere. It should be noted, however, that changes in the administration of some locally-based institutions may be increasingly important in influencing the future of these institutions. With the diminishing role of the Catholic Church in maintaining local hospitals, colleges, and even certain recreational activities, and governmental acceptance of responsibilities for overseeing such services, there may be a decreased range of institutions found locally.

Although many needs of villagers are filled locally, the area is not "institutionally complete" or characterized by "closure." Within the region there are a number of English Canadians; furthermore, even in areas such as Shippegan where there have been relatively few anglophones, the importance of anglophone "bosses" has probably always outranked their numerical strength.

Villagers are members of activity fields which include representatives of the English-speaking world. In dealings with the government, as in dealings with some fish buying companies, village bilinguals act as intermediaries between monolingual francophones and monolingual anglophone representatives of the outside world.

In short, when contacts could be made with English Canadians who permanently reside in the area, or who may be fishing or working in the area, such contacts are minimized; religious, residential, and kin channels of communication and incorporation effectively restrict entrance of strangers into the inner core of village life. As Barth succinctly stated,

> stable inter-ethnic relations presuppose such a
> structuring of interaction: a set of prescriptions
> governing situations of contact, and allowing for
> articulating in some sectors or domains of activity,
> and a set of proscriptions on social situations
> preventing inter-ethnic interaction in other sectors,

and thus insulating parts of the cultures from confrontation and modification (1969a:16).

When contacts must be made with Anglo-Canadians or with those of Anglo-dominated institutions or areas, a bilingual buffers the contact of the monolinguals on either side; by such a maneuver most villagers need never learn English. Villagers remain monolingual French-speakers not because there is an absence of anglophones with whom contact might be made, or with whom it must be made, but because there is an intermediary insulating the contact.

In sum, isolation per se does not account for the lack of bilingualism and lack of English language adoption among villagers; the particular sociocultural patterns which channel and buffer inter-ethnic contacts also importantly contribute to the lack of English language learning and French language loss among villagers of Ste. Marie-sur-Mer. Among factors contributing to the villagers' ethnic persistence are: attitudes which discourage contacts with strangers in general and Anglo-Canadians in particular and which stem from the nature of the historical relations between Acadians and English Canadians; positive attitudes which villagers hold toward themselves as Acadians and which encourage the maintenance of ties with fellow Acadians; regional demography, settlement patterns, and historical, as well as contemporary, exploitation of resources; and specific features of village life discussed in the preceding chapters.

ACADIAN ETHNICITY

In his discussions of the ethnic identity and the ethnic group boundaries of Pathans in Afghanistan, Barth suggested that ethnic identity can be characterized by essential attributes. Features of Pathan life style reflect intra-group variation according to the political and economic situations in which the Pathans are found; the life style does not define ethnic group boundaries nor is it essential to ethnic identity. Barth wrote

> such diversities of life style do not appear significantly to impair the Pathans' self-image as a characteristic and distinctive ethnic unit with unambiguous social and distributional boundaries. Thus the cultural diversity which we observe between different Pathan communities, and which objectively seems to be of an order of magnitude comparable to that between any such community and neighboring non-Pathan groups, does not provide criteria for differentiating persons in terms of ethnic identity. On the contrary, members of this society select only certain cultural traits, and make these the unambiguous criteria for ascription to the ethnic group (1969b:119).

Barth has distinguished between characteristics for "self-ascription and ascription by others," which define group boundaries, and "morphological characteristics," or "culture traits," which may be associated with ethnic groups, but which do not define the boundaries of those groups; that is, he has distinguished between ethnic groups and "culture-bearing units" (1969a:11-15). Barth asserted that equating ethnic groups with culture-bearing units, and delineating ethnic groups in terms of culture traits, create two difficulties in identifying group boundaries. First, certain culture traits associated with an ethnic group today may have not been associated with the group in the past; and variation in ecological adaptation may create differences in culture traits between contemporaneous communities of the same ethnic group. In both cases, cultural diversity does not indicate that ethnic identities are different, but simply that culture traits associated with the ethnic group are different. Thus, Barth suggests that culture traits, morphological characteristics, or life styles per se, are unreliable indicators of group boundaries and ethnic identity. Rather, ethnic identity should be defined in terms of basic attributes which have had continuing importance through time and in all the regional contexts in which the local communities of the group are found.

Attributes of Acadian Ethnicity

Barth's approach is useful for characterizing Acadian ethnicity and in accounting for variation in Acadian life styles at the local levels.

There are four attributes essential to Acadian ethnicity: historical origins of the Acadian people, Roman Catholicism, the French language (particularly its Acadian dialects), and contemporary residence in the Maritime Provinces. Each of these four attributes is necessary, though none individually is sufficient, for purposes of ascription and self-ascription of Acadians. All four attributes have been discussed at various points in preceding chapters. Here I will make just a few additional summary comments.

First, Acadians distinguish themselves not only from Anglo-Canadians, but also from other French Canadian populations. Acadians share many culture traits with French Canadians elsewhere in Canada; however, Acadians constitute a separate ethnic group because they see themselves as different from other French Canadians and are recognized as different by French Canadians. The origins of this separateness in identity and identification have a long history, and dialect differences, descent from eighteenth century exiled Acadians, and residence in the Maritimes today are the attributes important in ascription and self-ascription of individuals as Acadians rather than as French Canadians.

Acadians are also distinguished from Anglo-Canadians of the region. Although Ste. Marie and Anglo-Canadian outports in Newfoundland share many culture traits, the Acadian language, religion, and "origin myth" (in this case true) of the <u>grand dérangement</u> and descent from the eighteenth century Acadians, serve to clearly distinguish Acadians from Anglo-Canadians in rural maritime communities.

Barth suggests that features defining an ethnic group's boundary receive varying amounts of emphasis by the members involved; "some cultural features are used by the actors as signals and emblems of differences, others are ignored, and in some relationships radical differences are played down and denied" (1969a:14). Today the attribute emphasized by Acadians is French language use. Within the Maritime Provinces, the ability to speak French usually is taken to indicate that an individual is a francophone and of French Canadian origins. Hence, anyone who speaks French, or who speaks English and French, is assumed to be of French origins. Dialect differences identify a French-speaking individual as being from Quebec, Europe, or the Maritime Provinces. Thus, language use and language abilities are the most important diacritica of Acadian identity for they clearly mark off Acadians from both anglophones and francophones elsewhere in Canada.

Acadians emphasize the importance of language in relation to ethnic identity in a number of ways. For example, educated Acadians, especially, may use the Acadian dialect to demonstrate their origins and identity; folk song writers carefully include

Acadian themes such as the sea and fishing, and use uniquely Acadian phrases and words; periodical letters to the editor of l'Évangéline are written in a style similar to a phonetic transcription of Acadian speech. In short, language is important to Acadians not only in relation to maintaining or winning certain basic language rights (e.g., the right to be served a summons in either French or English), but in relation to the role language plays in distinguishing Acadians from both Anglo-Canadians and other French Canadians.

Although the four attributes of Acadian ethnicity are general and basic to ethnicity in Acadian society, in different local contexts the attributes have varying kinds of importance. These attributes, as values common to all Acadians, are manifest in different ways. Thus, for example, villagers of Ste. Marie value the Acadian dialect as something which is unique and it is the only dialect some villagers command. They are proud of their dialect which they describe as containing the "old" and "pure" words of French. On the other hand, among the educated Acadians of Moncton, the Acadian dialect is not so much revered and used but it is still maintained as a group symbol; although educated Acadians may be able to use the dialect, they may do so only in contexts in which ethnic solidarity or identity is being demonstrated. In general, the more fundamental language issue for French speakers in Moncton has been the right to use _any_ French dialect in certain public contexts.

Hence, the specific meaning of each attribute associated with ethnicity varies according to the local setting. The meaning of the attributes will vary according to such factors as the historical relationships between the two ethnic groups in the local setting,

ETHNIC PERSISTENCE 167

the proportion of each ethnic group represented, and the relative power which each of the groups holds.

Life Style and the Structuring of Contacts

Preceding chapters have described the life style of villagers in Ste. Marie for the purpose of accounting for their ethnic persistence; the life style in Ste. Marie can now be considered for the purpose of suggesting general connections between life style in local settings, structuring of contacts, and persistence.

Briefly, the life style of Acadians in Ste. Marie derives its major characteristics from patterns associated with residence, religion, and kinship. Within these three realms, there is considerable homogeneity and overlap in activities and behavior. For example, the neighborhood is largely composed of interrelated families; ideal behavior within the neighborhood is thus often that of kin behavior; the obligations and duties associated with kin roles are given definition and reinforcement by the Church.

The residents of the local community are homogeneous in their ethnic origins, religion, language, and in their dependence on, and involvement in, the fishery; this homogeneity creates a milieu in which residents have much the same interests and activities, and behavior associated with various roles is played out largely for the same audience. This latter characteristic of roles and relationships of villagers of Ste. Marie and the high proportion of francophones in the Shippegan area create few occasions for switching languages or ethnic identities; a villager has limited opportunities in which to speak English and advertently or inadvertently present himself as being an anglophone to a stranger. In various areas of the world where biculturalism or multiculturalism is prevalent, such switching or "cultural commuting" (van den Berghe 1970:146) is common and has been suggested to be a strategy employed for economic advantage (van den Berghe 1970).

It appears that in urban areas of New Brunswick where the proportion of anglophones to francophones is equal or substantially higher, language switching by francophones is usual, e.g., salesclerks in the Moncton area can appear to be either francophone or anglophone with apparent ease. Careful examination of such situations is needed to ascertain whether only languages are being switched by bilingual persons or whether a fuller code representing a total ethnic identity is being switched by bicultural persons. It would appear that such switching or lack of switching represents an important difference between villagers of Ste. Marie, who, as members of an intermediate society, are nearly always francophone and those elsewhere in the province or in Maritime Canada who, as members of a complex society, may have both abilities and occasions in which they present themselves as either francophone or anglophone.

In the milieu in which villagers of Ste. Marie live, ethnic persistence has been encouraged and I found no indication that the persistence of villagers as Acadians is weakening. The use of the English language is negligible; most people regularly perform their obligations as Catholics and appear to be strong in religious convictions. Villagers express a knowledge of themselves as being part of an Acadian people, and as possessing a history and heritage which has unfolded over several centuries in the Maritime Provinces.

One might ask, however, what are the effects of persistence when different morphological characteristics, or life styles, exist in other Acadian communities or regions? How is persistence effected when life styles are different from those described in Ste. Marie? To illustrate the potential variation I will consider religion and residence as influences on persistence.

The parish has considerable importance in incorporating rural Acadians and strengthening their bonds. However, the nature of the parish in urban areas in French Canada is different from what I described for the parish of St. Raphael. Urban parishes in Quebec do not always correspond to territorial units; all those who live within the territory of the parish may not attend that parish church, and all those who attend the parish church may not live within that parish (Falardeau 1949). Hence, the importance of the urban parish in reinforcing the solidarity of a local residential group is potentially weaker than that described for the rural parish in the Shippegan area. I suspect that urban parishes (such as in Moncton) are different from rural parishes with regard to their importance in incorporation and solidifying ties of Acadians. Thus, I am suggesting that the parish, as a morphological characteristic affecting persistence, varies in importance and function according to the context in which it is found. Specifically, rural parishes are more important than urban ones in incorporating Acadian people and in intensifying the bonds between them.

Urban parishes may include both francophones and anglophones. In such cases although different Masses are said for each language group, membership in a common parish may increase inter-ethnic contacts and encourage the creation of mixed marriages.

Thus, the importance of homogeneity (or heterogeneity) in the ethnic composition of the local community and parish influences persistence; the amount of overlap between territorial units in which individuals interact has a similar influence. These, and other, variables have been suggested by Vallee (1969; 1971) and Tremblay (1961) as influences on Acadian acculturation or persistence. This study has shown that the variables are relevant to an understanding of persistence of Acadians in Ste. Marie, but additional studies in various local settings are needed to test the relative importance, or weight, that should be attached to each of the variables.

The bilingual intermediary plays an important role in the structuring of inter-ethnic contacts. In Ste. Marie, the few bilingual intermediaries are integral to the life style of the village, but their bilingualism is not an indicator of acculturation; rather, in Ste. Marie this bilingualism encourages persistence of monolingualism among the wider village population. The role of bilinguals may be to channel acculturative influences into the local community, or to buffer and dilute acculturative influences; the role of bilinguals in Acadian society could be profitably studied in various local settings.

In short, I suggest the following connections between life style and persistence, societal ethnicity and local ethnicity: At a societal level, ethnicity comprises essential and basic attributes which are valid and applicable within individual local groups.

Though local communities share a basic ethnic identity and define group boundaries in the same way, the manner in which boundaries are maintained in local settings are quite different. The life style, or the morphological characteristics of the local group (e.g., bilinguals as intermediaries between two ethnic groups, institutions which incorporate members of one group and exclude those of another group), determine how boundaries are maintained. Life style does not define ethnic boundaries, but it does influence the ways in which boundaries are maintained.

ETHNIC BOUNDARIES AND CONFLICT IN NEW BRUNSWICK

The culture traits or life style associated with an ethnic group may change through time and may differ according to ecological demands of different locales (Barth 1969a:11-13). The latter variation may be seen in the fact that Acadian fishermen of coastal villages in New Brunswick appear to have as many culture traits in common with Anglo-Canadian fishermen of Newfoundland's outports as they do with urban-dwelling francophone elites in Moncton. Similar techno-environmental adaptations of fishermen in the two provinces have resulted in the parallel development of features relating to economic and domestic life (for example, crew composition, crew recruitment, and village settlement patterns).

Earlier I indicated that the life style of rural Acadians has altered through time, and especially during the years of this century. Though the essential attributes demarcating Acadian ethnicity have remained constant through the years, different attributes appear to have held more importance than others during

particular periods. It also appears that the major attribute
which defined ethnic group boundaries also defined the nature of
conflict between Acadians and British or Anglo-Canadians during
different periods.

The attributes which have historically defined Acadian ethnic
group boundaries related to political rights of Acadian residents
in the region, to religion, and to language. All three attributes
served to demarcate Acadians from others of the colony of Nova
Scotia in the eighteenth century. However, political allegiance
and the nature of rights as citizens of the region were the important
factors underlying the conflict between Acadians and British
authorities during this early period. Schemes to introduce French-
speaking Protestant colonists into the Acadian lands with the goal
of their mixing and marrying with the French-speaking Acadians were
instigated with the hope of assuring Acadian political allegiance
(MacNutt 1965:37). Vowing allegiance to the English monarch,
not changing religion per se, was the repeated demand made
of Acadians. The conflict finally culminated in the forced exile
of Acadians from the area. Even after the Acadians were permitted
reentry to the area following the Treaty of Paris in 1763, the conditions under which they were allowed to return included a stipulation requiring them to swear allegiance to the English monarch
(MacNutt 1965:62).

In the latter part of the eighteenth century and early part of
the nineteenth, religious affiliation was the important attribute
distinguishing Acadians from most Anglo-Canadians. Catholics were
given the right to vote in New Brunswick in 1784, but they were not

allowed to be elected to the colony's Assembly. It was not until 1830 that Catholics of New Brunswick were given the right to elect representatives who were themselves Catholic (Garner 1953:214). Religion continued to be a source of contention throughout the nineteenth century; questions relating to the religious affiliation of teachers and religious subjects to be taught were the basis for further conflict between Acadians and Anglo-Canadians. By the provincial Common Schools Act, passed in 1871, schools were to be "non-sectarian and use texts prescribed by the provincial Board of Education" (Thorburn 1961:31-35). The considerable controversy over the bill resulted in its eventual modification which permitted Acadians to maintain control over their schools. This meant that nuns were often used as teachers and that religious subjects, emblems, prayers, etc., were assured a place in the schools.

The twentieth century brought confrontations between Acadians and Anglo-Canadians over language rights and use. Conflict within the Catholic Church itself stemmed from this question during the latter half of the nineteenth century and early part of the twentieth. Although Acadians in some areas of the province were assigned priests who were French-speaking, and often Acadian, there were other francophones in the province who were denied French-speaking priests. After much concerted effort and appeals to individuals high in the Roman Catholic church hierarchy, Irish, English-speaking priests were generally replaced by Acadian, French-speaking priests. It was not until 1910 that the first French-speaking bishop was appointed in New Brunswick. Eventually the province was divided into four dioceses, three of which today are headed by French-speaking bishops. English-speaking priests today are stationed only in areas where there is a large enough congregation of English-speaking Catholics to warrant their presence.

This whole struggle within the Catholic Church regarding language use is a reflection of the type of struggle which took place in other provincial institutions, including schools. In the schools problems relating to language use in teaching, assistance by the provincial government in providing books, teacher training facilities for French speakers, creation of special curricula for francophones, etc., have only recently begun to be resolved satisfactorily for Acadians. A French-language teacher training school and a French-language university have been created; there are also several vocational training schools in which French is the working language. In areas in which the two major ethnic groups are numerically equal, or in which the French-speaking group is relatively small, the adequacy of French-language educational facilities varies. Some areas have separate schools for the two language groups; other areas have bilingual schools where some classes are in French and others in English.

In short, during the last 250 years three attributes in combination have been important in triggering conflict between Acadians and their English-speaking neighbors, but the prominence of each has shifted at different periods. In broad terms, the issue of political allegiance was particularly important in the eighteenth century, religion was important in the nineteenth century, and language became important in the twentieth century. Although the essential defining attributes of Acadian ethnicity have remained the same over the course of nearly three centuries, particular conflict issues at given periods resulted in the emphasis of one attribute over the others.

Today French Canadian sociologists have defined the differences between New Brunswick's anglophones and francophones as being one of class, with francophones occupying the lower socioeconomic strata and anglophones occupying the higher (see above, pp. 22-26). They describe Acadians as being dominated by Anglo-Canadians and encourage Acadians to confront and change the nature of this relationship. Here emerging areas of conflict are based on a feature which Acadian leaders have chosen to emphasize--differences in socioeconomic power and wealth.

Additional community, regional, and societal studies in New Brunswick are needed to provide a fuller picture of inter-ethnic relations in the province. The study of the structure of contacts between Acadians and Anglo-Canadians provides one useful approach toward understanding inter-ethnic relations and persistence of Acadians in the province. Furthermore, inter-ethnic group conflict may be profitably examined through consideration of attributes defining ethnic group boundaries.

POSTSCRIPT
1984

The description of Ste. Marie-sur-Mer and the Shippegan area given in the preceding chapters focuses on the maintenance of ethnic group boundaries and the pervasive influence of the fishery. Local people have two major sources of identity, one involving ethnicity and one involving the conditions of their livelihood. Though both sources of identity are important and can be intertwined, as reflected in the <u>Marc Guylaine</u> affair, they have varying degrees of salience according to the context in which the respective identities are emphasized and manipulated (see Davis 1977).

The cultural continuity of Acadians has been traditionally attributed to their isolation from anglophones, but I suggested that Acadians' contact with at least some anglophones or anglophone-dominated institutions is inevitable. Though Acadians predominate in the Shippegan area, anglophones and anglophone institutions have traditionally played important economic and political roles there. Following Barth (1969), I suggested that, under such circumstances, cultural means of maintaining boundaries through processes of incorporation and exclusion importantly contribute to cultural continuity and Acadian survival. Furthermore, I indicated that the features setting off Acadians from others have changed historically

POSTSCRIPT 177

and that there had been attempts to intentionally alter those features according to political expedience.

The reliance on the fishery (both fishing and the processing of fish) entails considerable hardship with often only modest returns. There is little romance in being exposed to the often harsh conditions at sea and the unpleasant working conditions of the <u>usines</u>, in encountering frequent danger, in knowing that those one loves may be encountering danger, and in receiving seasonal and uncertain income. But for most people who live in the Shippegan area, employment opportunities are limited to those of the fishery. Because of these and other socioeconomic problems in northeastern New Brunswick, the federal and provincial governments had targeted the area for economic and social development in the mid-1960s. Various programs affecting education, transportation, and the fishery were underway in the early 1970s when fieldwork was done.

In assessing change in village and regional life over the last ten years, the observation <u>plus ça change, plus le même chose</u> is appropriate. Events have not resulted in, or reflected, radical change. Various important issues in the larger society remain unresolved and accordingly this is reflected in uncertainty at the village level. But some examples might best illustrate these points.

THE FISHERY

As indicated in earlier chapters, the village and the Shippegan area have become progressively affected by government intervention.

One area where that intervention has been most important is the fishery. The most significant fisheries-related action by the Canadian government in the last ten years has been the declaration of a 200-mile limit in 1977, within which exploitation of ocean resources are to be controlled by Canada. This presents the opportunity for comprehensive management of the East Coast fishery. If skillfully and carefully managed, the offshore fishery and fish processing firms on the mainland might be able to expand their operations and absorb labor heretofore inefficiently employed in the inshore fishery. However, because of the depressed economy and high unemployment in Atlantic Canada, the danger exists that expanded operations may attract unemployed people from other than the coastal communities and the inshore fishery work force may maintain its current numbers, excessive for the fish stocks available. Thus, the inshore fishery could remain inefficient and characterized by low returns to fishermen (Copes 1978, 1979; Mitchell 1978; Prattis 1981).

Though restructuring and rationalizing of the Atlantic coastal fishery as a result of the implementation of the 200-mile limit is important to all regional fishermen, it is less significant for fishermen of the Gulf of St. Lawrence than for fishermen in Nova Scotia and Newfoundland. Foreign fleets had not been competing with Gulf fishermen for stocks, and so new restrictions on their activities benefit Gulf fishermen little, if at all (Copes 1978: 167).

Shippegan area fishermen exploit the Gulf waters, and the effects of the 200-mile limit for them are thus indirect rather

than direct. An indirect effect of the limit and the renewed
concern for careful management of the ocean resources will be
the increasing scrutiny by government officials concerned with the
efficient exploitation of fish stocks. Scrutiny of the Lameque-
Shippegan fishery would reveal increasing differences between the
profits and earnings of the inshore fishery versus those in the
mid-water fishery and offshore fishery[1] and would raise serious
questions regarding the viability of the inshore fishery. In
1969, the average incomes of many inshore fishermen and offshore
crew members were not significantly different (Charron 1972).
However, in 1979 average earnings for selected inshore fishermen
in the Lameque-Shippegan area were found to be only one-quarter
(or less) those of mid-water and offshore captains and crew.
Inshore captains averaged earnings of $5,250 while captains
averaged $22,685 on vessels fishing crab, $19,053 on Scottish
seiners, and $57,386 on herring seiners. Helpers on inshore
boats had an average income of $4,402, while deckhands averaged
$20,497 on vessels fishing crab, $19,053 on Scottish seiners,
and $25,730 on herring seiners (Dugas:1980, Table 11).

In the absence of a significant increase in the market price
for fish, particularly lobster on which inshore fishermen rely
heavily,[2] or in the absence of increased catches, the inshore
fishery and the people who depend upon it will continue to need
extensive government subsidization. Size of lobster catches per
fishing boat might be increased through the further reduction
of the numbers of inshore fishermen and the elimination of illegal
lobster fishing. The first strategy would be extremely unpopular,

considering the lack of alternative employment available, and the second has proven extremely difficult to do. The future of the inshore fishery appears precarious if nothing is done and whatever may be done will have implications for local people's identity as based in their livelihood. At stake are the lives of inshore fishermen, severely disrupted if they are forced to seek other employment, increasingly impoverished if they are not.

Incomes cited above for participants in the mid-water and offshore fisheries might suggest that all is well in these fisheries and in the processing industry which depends upon them. But such is not the case. For example, in the summer of 1984 the crab quota was being met too rapidly in the season, with usine workers having large catches to process in a short period of time. The seasonal work period for the latter workers was going to be so short that they would not qualify for unemployment insurance payments, which require a minimum qualification period of 10 weeks' work. Without U.I. payments, these people would face a winter without income. To combat the problem, a system of quotas per vessel per week was instituted late in the season to slow down the fishing and the supplying of crabs to the usines. The system was reported to be less than satisfactory, however, for usine workers were still experiencing a reduction in hours of work, which would lessen the U.I. payments received in winter as well.

The situation discussed above illustrates the problems in the fishery which deny easy solution.[3] Fish quotas are needed to prevent overfishing and the destruction of resources; however, fish quotas can reduce the present incomes (and later U.I. payments)

of fishermen and of the work-force at usines. Work in usines still
remains one of the most important sources of employment in the
Shippegan area. Two-thirds of all employed women and a quarter of
all employed men in the parish work in the processing plants
(Statistics Canada 1984).

In spite of the continuing problems in the fishery, the Shippegan
area now exhibits the appearance of material prosperity. Highways
have been improved and shopping facilities expanded. New housing
has sprung up in all the villages and along many roads which had
been previously unsettled. Nearly half of all private dwellings
in Shippegan Parish have been built since 1971; only a third of such
dwellings in the province as a whole were built in the same period
(Statistics Canada 1984). Ste. Marie has seen a proliferation of
new bungalows along the coastal road and along the new inland
streets running perpendicular to the shore.[4] The boundaries of the
original land holdings in the village have become progressively
blurred with the increased division of land and house construction.
Neighborhoods are no longer kin-based enclaves, for some of the new
household heads are "strangers," unrelated to others in the neighborhood and village. Old restrictions regarding purchase of land
by outsiders are apparently no more.

Although the Shippegan area has the look of prosperity, that
appearance is misleading, for individual earnings continue to be substantially lower than those in the province. Parish men and women
each earn only about two-thirds that of men and women in the province
as a whole ($8,991:$13,580 and $4,480:$6,968 for men and women
respectively). Thus, although the average family income in the

parish ($19,679) is 93 percent of that in the province (Statistics Canada 1984), more than two incomes per most families are needed to approach that provincial average.

The importance of multiple incomes in parish families is reflected in the high incidence of married women who work; 62 percent of the married women in the parish are employed, in comparison to the 46 percent of married women who are employed in the province as a whole (Statistics Canada 1984). Parish women's employment continues to generate smaller incomes than those of men. For example, only 2 percent of employed women, but 17 percent of employed men, earned more than $15,000 in 1981. Development strategies in the area have focused on the fishery. Within the fishery women's employment is confined to work in usines, which provides small incomes in comparison to those received by at least some men in fishing crews (see Davis 1981; 1983). On the basis of the several salaries and transfer payments received by families, a new standard of living and "style of consumption" (Runciman 1969:48) is enjoyed, but that should not obscure the fact that individual incomes of many people, particularly women, remain exceptionally low.

Also apparent are the increasing differences within the area in incomes and the resulting standards of living they provide; differences in incomes here are more pronounced than in the province as a whole. In the province, 37 percent of employed men earn $15,000 or more, however only 17 percent of Shippegan Parish men earn that amount. Furthermore, in New Brunswick 11 percent of employed men earn $25,000 or more, while in the parish only 4 percent do so (Statistics Canada 1984). Although these comparisons indicate yet again that parish incomes are on average lower than provincial ones, they also indicate a sharper delineation between those with low or modest incomes and those with high incomes in the parish.

GROUP SOLIDARITY AND INTER-ETHNIC GROUP RELATIONS

Above I have characterized change in the fishery as being developmental rather than radical. The potential for increasing differentiation between incomes generated in the fishery was present ten years ago, and the viability of some aspects of the fishery was questioned ten years ago. Many residents of the village were part of an "underground economy" even then; their pluralistic work activities were necessary as incomes generated in the fishery were insufficient. Women had always contributed to the labor of the household economy, even if they had rarely received wages for their work. Certain other aspects of the economy in the area, and by extrapolation elsewhere, may yet have important consequences for Acadian group solidarity.

First, however, I shall consider how events of a sociolinguistic and political nature have affected that solidarity and inter-ethnic group relations in New Brunswick. The francophone population in the province continues to be characterized by fragmentation and competition, each region guarding its distinctiveness. Residents of Madawaska County (located in the northwestern part of the province and bordering Quebec) continue to stress that they are not Acadian and that they have their own needs and interests. But more telling is the continued division within the Acadian population itself. Old divisions between those in the Moncton area and those on the North Shore-Acadian Peninsula continue to resurface. Most recent has been the conflict over the location of the new French-language daily newspaper, a replacement for the defunct l'Évangéline, with both Moncton and Caraquet being proposed as locations. The lack of cooperation in the matter is ostensibly based on differences of principle. The Moncton group is to receive financial assistance from the provincial government. The North Shore group considers such financial support to be accompanied by government attempts to control the new paper. Consequently, the two groups will not join forces. However, the conflict also reflects and reinforces long-standing political competition between the two Acadian regions. It is highly doubtful that two daily French-language newspapers can be sustained by the New Brunswick francophone readership alone. But francophones on Prince Edward Island and in Nova Scotia are not enthusiastic about supporting newspapers based in New Brunswick. The lack of cooperation--within and without the province--may mean that no daily French-language newspaper has a reasonable chance for survival.

Francophones in different provincial regions have their own local institutions and groups through which they act; they are not united under one set of institutions. However, there is not a full complement of institutions and services in individual areas. The Société des Acadiens du Nouveau Brunswick (S.A.N.B.) has recently proposed a new "social contract" in which "separate, but equal" government institutions and services would be provided for both language groups. The division of the Department of Education into separate sub-departments to serve francophones and anglophones is the type of division which is desired in all government departments.

POSTSCRIPT

Although suggested in order to ensure that francophones have access to government services parallel to those available to anglophones, their provision would also ensure uniformity in at least some institutions and services all francophone areas enjoy.

The proposal has consequences for inter-ethnic group relations. It has received some negative response from anglophones in the province, similar to the reaction to government bilingualism policies in Western Canada and, to a lesser degree, in Ontario. Often where there are large numbers of Canadians who are other than francophone or anglophone, heated resistence to the special status of French Canadians is particularly apt to occur. Multiculturalism, giving French Canadians no more than the same status as all other non-British ethnic groups, is advocated by many immigrants and descendants of recent immigrants. They see their own ethnic heritage as devalued in comparison to the special status given French Canadians (Wardhaugh 1983:198-218).

As already indicated, New Brunswick has relatively few residents who are neither francophone nor anglophone, and this may lessen the "backlash" to the provincial bilingualism policy. However, important in New Brunswick is the not uncommon anglophone perception that requirements of bilingualism in the government civil service deny them the opportunity to compete for needed jobs. Similarly, any alteration in the government administration of services which could be perceived as resulting in additional cost to the tax payers undoubtably would be unpopular among many anglophones. In short, the provincial government will find it easier to agree to the general notion of separate services for francophones than to provide them.

SOCIOECONOMIC DIFFERENCES AND ETHNIC GROUP SOLIDARITY

The events described above reflect continuing problems regarding francophone regionalism and the strategies employed to ensure the maintenance and growth of the francophone population in the province. Economic differentiation within the population also has consequences for group maintenance and growth, both at the local or village level and at the regional and provincial level. I will begin by considering the latter first.

At the provincial level, emerging socioeconomic differences may fragment the Acadian population in ways to rival the long-standing regional divisions. For example, I suspect that people in the Shippegan area may not be so immediately concerned about the provision of separate francophone institutions and services as they are about the problems of making a reasonable living. The priority of their concerns may not be the same as others in the francophone population who, because of their education and occupations, have secure and comfortable incomes. Similarly, the difficulty experienced by the S.A.N.B. in attempting to create active regional councils throughout the province may partially reflect the inability to bridge the gap between the "bread and butter" issues immediately relevant to local people and the structural changes in the province which may be needed to improve local life over the long run. Just as regional differences have inhibited province-wide mobilization of francophones in the past, socioeconomic differences may do so in the future.

In places like Ste. Marie, increasing income differences, along with the increased presence of heretofore barred "strangers," may alter quite fundamentally the nature of local life. Ties of kinship, religion, and long association in communities have previously overcome or neutralized the potential divisiveness of income differences. Now long association between those in such communities is not assured, and religion is reported to have less influence today. Villagers indicate that they have increasing difficulty getting some children to attend Mass, and marital separations and divorces are more common. Birth rates have also fallen, suggesting a greater secular approach to family planning.[5] Kin ties will undoubtedly remain strong, but they will become less identified with ties between neighbors, villagers, or parishioners. Increasingly, language may become that component of Acadian ethnicity with which most villagers and, more generally, most Acadians can identify.

Unresolved is the future of the fishery, particularly the inshore fishery, and of the francophone community's position within the institutional structure of the province. These issues have relevance for many thousands of people and will be largely decided in offices in Ottawa, Fredericton, or Moncton, but it is in villages like Ste. Marie where the issues become lived experiences. Villagers and their ancestors have been resilient to imposed socioeconomic change, dramatically so to their exile two centuries ago. There is no reason to think they will not be similarly resilient in the future.

Map 1. Gloucester County, Northeastern New Brunswick, Showing Shippegan (Lameque) Island and Ste. Marie-sur-Mer.

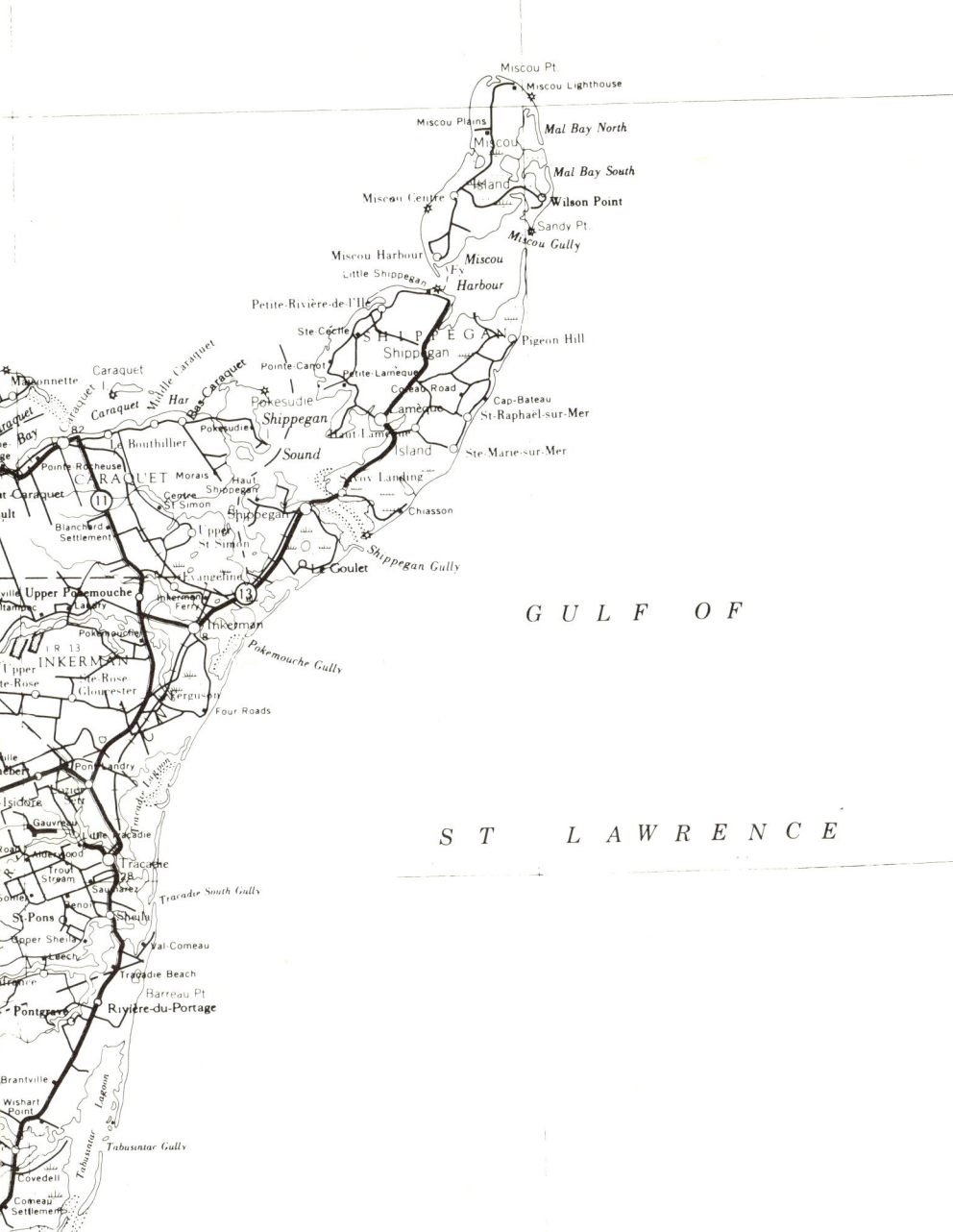

Source: Department of Energy, Mines and Resources, Canada.

Map 2. New Brunswick: Cities, Counties, Main Highways (#2, #8, #11), and Major Rivers

Source: Maritime Resource Management Service, Amherst, Nova Scotia.

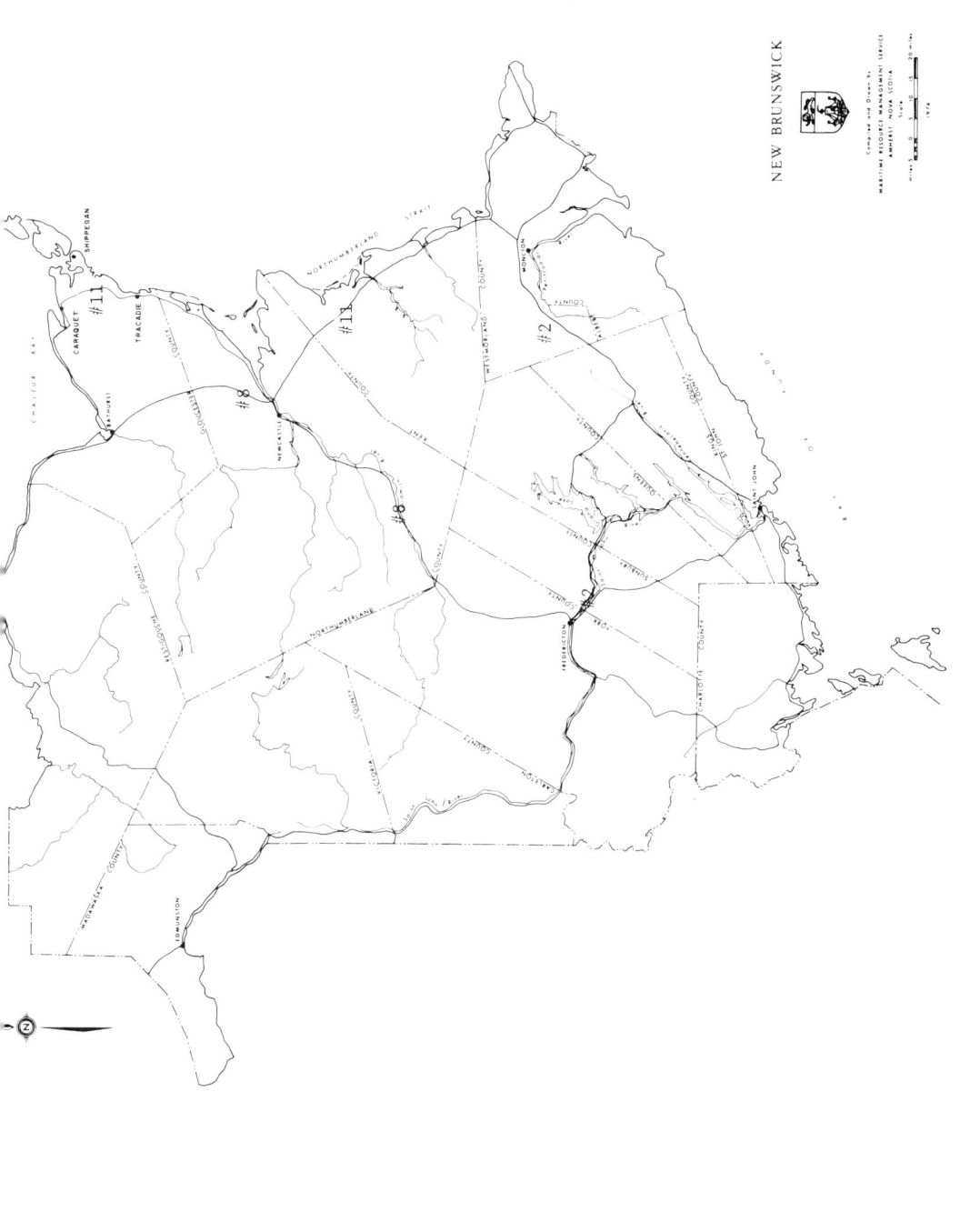

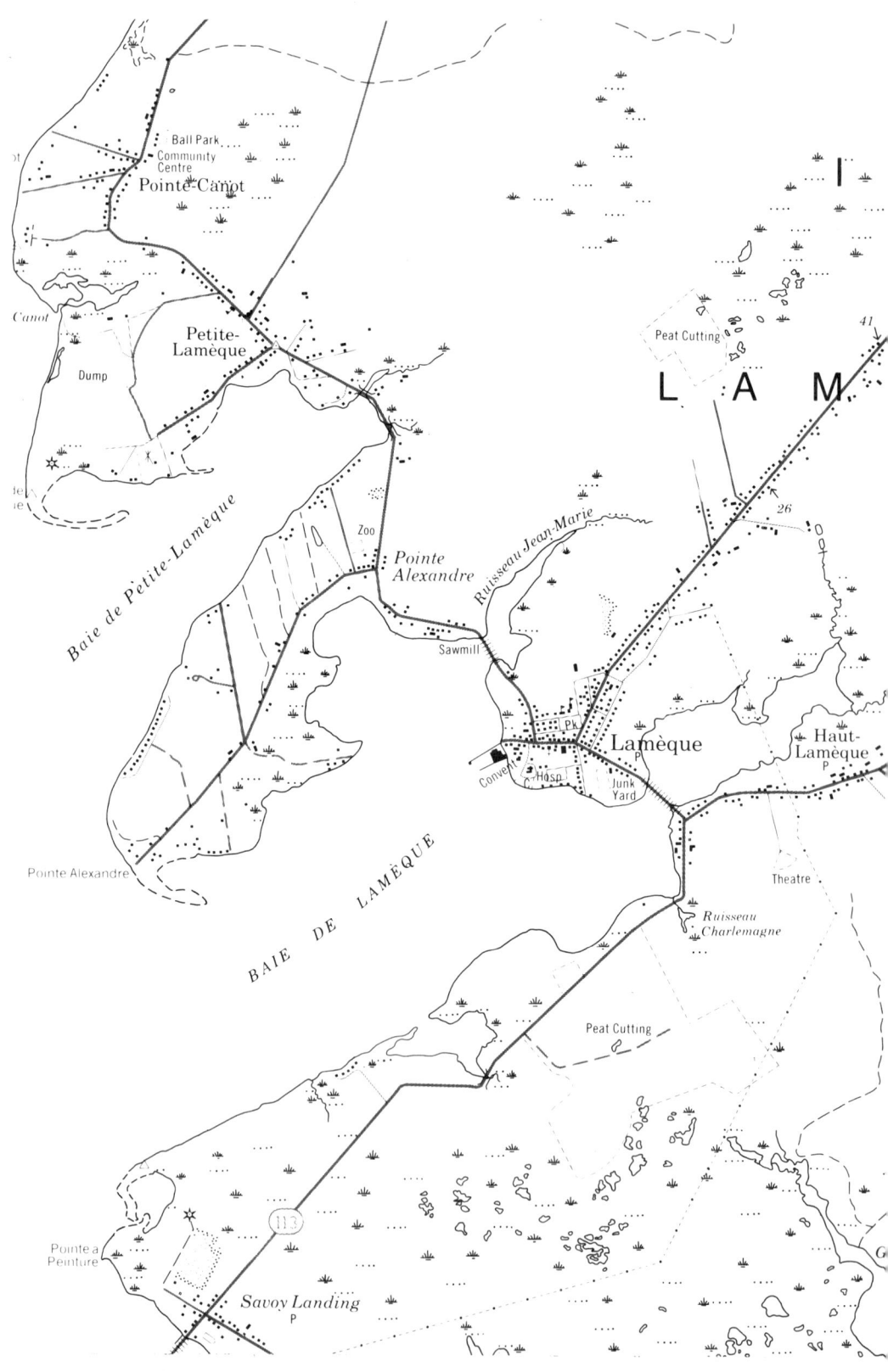

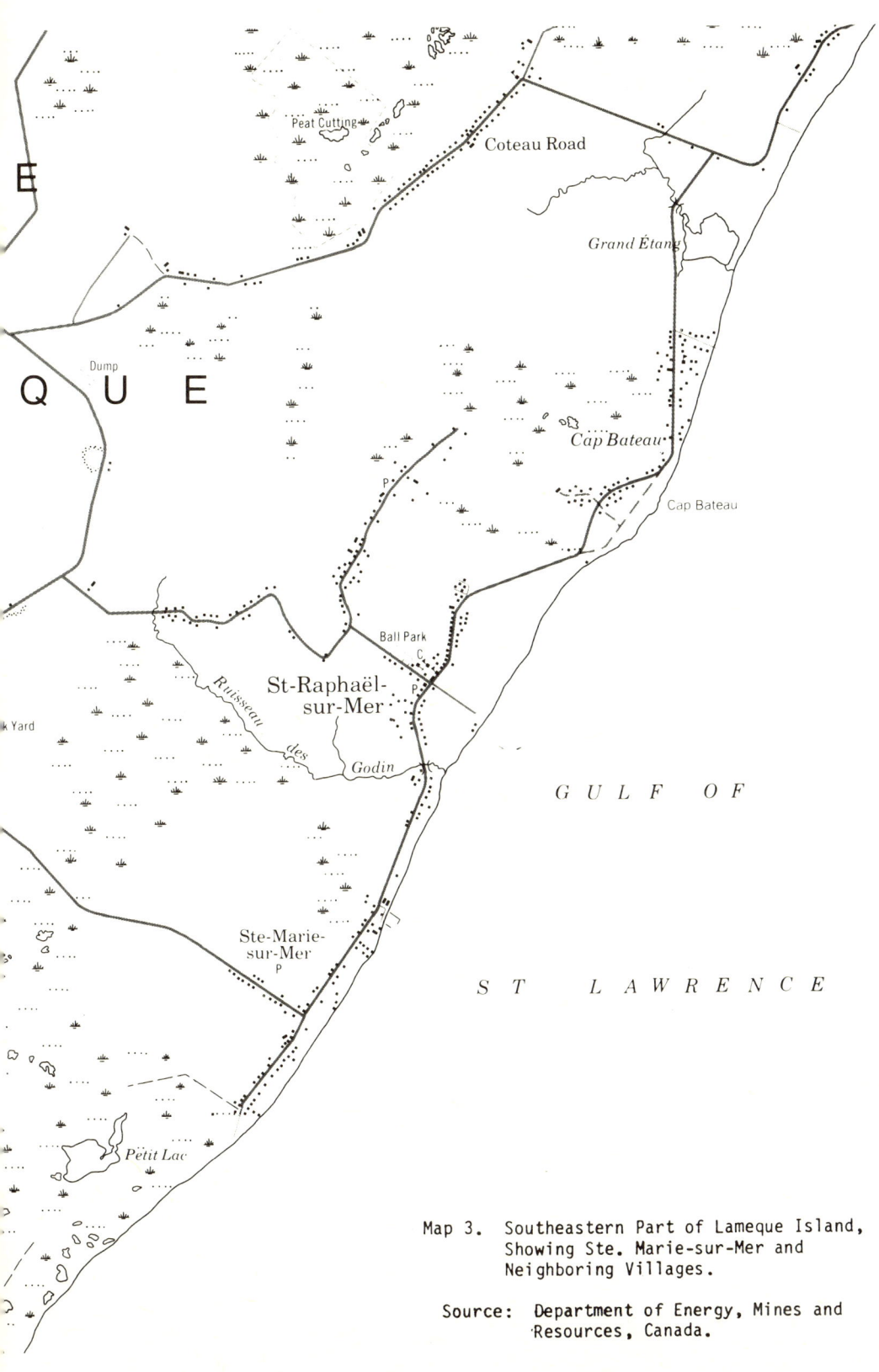

Map 3. Southeastern Part of Lameque Island, Showing Ste. Marie-sur-Mer and Neighboring Villages.

Source: Department of Energy, Mines and Resources, Canada.

APPENDIX

A further description of the circumstances surrounding the formation of the action group dealing with the Marc Guylaine affair will usefully illustrate the concerns of villagers and those of the region. Though conflict issues usually stem from a particular grievance, there are other associated matters which generally increase the seriousness of the immediate problem. When any grievance arises, several of the longstanding concerns of the local people resurface and reinforce the view that the government is yet again unconcerned about the villagers' problems.

The problems associated with the Marc Guylaine started six months before I began fieldwork when a herring seiner, the Lady Audette, sank with the loss of the crew. Five months later, a sister ship, the Lady Dorianne, also sank, taking three crewmen to their deaths. The circumstances under which the vessels had sunk were less than clear, and the affair was the major topic of concern among area residents. One of those fishermen lost in the sinkings had been from Ste. Marie, another had also been from the parish of St. Raphael, and several others were from the island. All nine victims were Acadian and from the North Shore of lower Gloucester County, from Lameque to Caraquet.

The particular aspect of the situation which triggered the call

APPENDIX 195

for a public meeting and the ensuing formation of the action group
related to the status of a third sister ship, the Marc Guylaine,
which was owned and operated by an islander and crewed by local
men. Strange circumstances were connected with the sinking of the
two ships, which in the case of the Lady Dorianne was described by
survivors as having taken place with the ship suddenly capsizing
and sinking; the captain and crew of the Marc Guylaine were afraid
to fish in the sister ship to the two lost vessels, and they termed
the ship a "floating coffin."

The whole affair remained unresolved in the middle of May, 1971,
a month after the second sinking. The immediate questions that
concerned local people were what was the cause of the two vessels'
sinking and was the Marc Guylaine seaworthy? By this time, antec-
dotes and rumors concerning various other aspects of the affair
composed much of local conversation. Stories regarding the
drownings of fishermen in past years were retold. Fishermen who
had lived through storms and the sinking of their ships recounted
their experience; many such men had "lost their nerve" to fish, and
it was believed that the survivors from the Lady Dorianne would
lose theirs too. Several of those who were lost in the two sinkings
were good swimmers, and the inevitability of their and everyone's
fate was mentioned in the discussions. In sum, the occasion of the
two sinkings provided a context in which the rigors, hardships, and
dangers of the fisherman's life were described and publicly
acknowledged. Local people are generally proud of their heritage
as fisherfolk, and the tragedies brought to public attention again

much of what this heritage involves and how this heritage sets fishermen and their families apart from others who work on the land.

Though it was generally assumed that the lost men had drowned and funeral Masses were said for them, there were others who suggested that the men weren't dead at all. Perhaps some strangers in a foreign ship had picked the men up, it was said, and the men would eventually be released and returned to their families. Such things had happened elsewhere, villagers explained, and perhaps it had happened with these men too. It was speculated that the widow of one fisherman would not remarry for she was convinced that the man was somewhere alive. Here, then, the concept of the stranger, the dangerous and unpredictable outsider, was being used by local people as a source of hope.

Most people, however, did accept the fact that the men were dead and that the circumstances under which one died were largely a matter of fate. Nevertheless, the people were not satisfied that the causes of the two sinkings were unrelated, which the government report had indicated. That is, the government certified that the ships had been seaworthy, that the Marc Guylaine was seaworthy, and there was no reason why the latter ship could not be immediately put back in use by the captain-owner. In essence, then, the government report suggested that the accidents had come about through human error, that the men fishing from the vessels had been at fault in not handling the ships properly. After the second sinking, the captain-owner of the Marc Guylaine had been sent a list of conditions which were necessary to be followed so that the vessel could be used safely. All but one of the seven conditions were

APPENDIX

considered by local fishermen to be impractical considering the structure and operation of the vessel; other conditions were considered ridiculous and insulting, for it appeared that the intelligence and competence of the fishermen were being questioned by the government, which reminded the fishermen to do such things as "watch for waves."

In general, the people concluded that the government did not care about the men who had drowned or about those men whose lives were endangered. They reasoned that more comprehensive tests would have been made by government officials if the affair was being taken seriously. The Marc Guylaine had been recently examined by federal Department of Transport officials, but the examination had been carried out in dry dock, instead of at sea under working conditions. The conclusion made locally was that this was just another example of how people of the region, French-speaking and traditionally supporters of the Liberal party, would never get attention from a Conservative government, then in power in the province. Thus, the situation provided reinforcement for the commonly accepted belief in the Shippegan area that only the Liberal party will look after the interests of French-speakers.

As the federal government in power was Liberal, another explanation had to be sought for the lack of attention given the affair at that level of government. Local people suggested that the government knew it had been at fault in approving the boat's design, and now the government was protecting itself from criticism and demands for financial compensation. Similarly, the firm which constructed the three vessels was suggested to have close ties with the pro-

vincial government and it was believed that the company was being
protected by the government. Local people thus reasoned that
somebody within the government had something to hide, and, hence,
the affair was being swept under some bureaucrat's rug. Money and
reputations were at stake, and the local people believed that it was
their money and their reputations (as fishermen) that were being
sacrificed to save the money and reputations of government officials
and their associates. Villagers feared that, as had happened in
the past, the interests of local Acadians would be ignored if they
conflicted with those of "big-shots" elsewhere, in this case
English-speaking shipbuilders and Conservative politicians from
southern New Brunswick.

Several of the issues raised regarding the Marc Guylaine affair
also involved the question of language use. Manuals of instruction
for the running and maintenance of the seiners were supposedly
supplied in English, though crewmen had only limited knowledge of
English. The list of conditions for the safe running of the
vessels had evidently been written in English and later translated into French. Local people found this translated copy foolish
and insulting, in the poor quality of the translation given. It
was suggested locally that either the person who translated the
document knew little French or the person writing the original
English document had known little about seiners. Much about the
Marc Guylaine affair illustrates the sensitivities and problems of
contemporary Acadians in New Brunswick, including those concerned
with ethnic relations. Not only were the Shippegan area people
being reminded in the affair that they were second-class citizens

in terms of language spoken, but their pride and heritage as fishermen were also threatened in the government intimations that the men had not known how to run the ships.

By mid-May the actions of interested individuals had not produced any tangible results in stirring the government into activity. Thus, those people most immediately involved called for a general meeting of all concerned, to be held at the community center in St. Raphael. The meeting was publicized in daily newspapers and, more importantly, it was mentioned in the weekend parish newsletter given out at Mass. This newsletter commonly contains reminders about meetings or events, and represents an effective way of spreading information to every parish household. As well, at Mass in St. Raphael, the priest called attention to the notice of the meeting to be held that afternoon.

Over 400 people from the Shippegan-Caraquet area attended the meeting. Many of the people attending were related to the lost crew members or to the crew and captain of the Marc Guylaine. Most people knew at least one of those who were lost or the families of the lost men. Thus the affair was being taken personally as famille and parenté were involved.

Individuals were appointed to maintain order in the meeting. A chairman and secretary to conduct the meeting were nominated, seconded, and elected by acclamation. The two men chosen, a merchant and a teacher, were local leaders in the Chambre de Commerce.

In the course of the meeting, several individuals made prepared statements in which they related the history of the tragedies and the various attempts made to instigate government investigation. Members of the audience participated by volunteering opinions and

asking questions. For example, one old fisherman rose to say that
clearly the three sister ships were poorly designed as the center
of gravity was too high. Another mentioned that the government
tests of the seaworthiness of the Marc Guylaine had not been done
at sea, but instead in dry dock; someone wondered if the officials
had feared to go to sea on the vessel. The captain of the Marc
Guylaine read the conditions for the safe operation of his vessel;
the conditions were met by outbursts of anger and outrage from the
audience who described them as ridiculous. Throughout the afternoon, the audience was noisily responsive in expressing approval or
disapproval about what had transpired concerning the affair.

One man rose and said that recently in Quebec there had been a
disaster similar to that regarding the three ships, only the Quebec
provincial government had immediately investigated the affair and
had assisted the people in all ways. The man asserted that the
people in New Brunswick were being given poor treatment. I do not
know if this was a local man making the comparison, or if he was
an outsider. However, his comment was received without comment
from the audience; there was neither agreement nor disagreement
with the man, and the topic was not pursued. I consider this to
be an example of the reaction local people generally give toward
those who present Quebec as the haven for French-speakers, including
Acadians. Local people recognize that they suffer disadvantages
in being French-speakers in a largely English-speaking province.
But, many local Acadians have also experienced discrimination at
the hands of Quebeckers.

Everyone in the audience was given the opportunity to contribute
to the discussion; one provincial politician (an Acadian and a

APPENDIX 201

Liberal Party member) was in attendance, and he pledged his support in resolving the affair. He received loud applause.

The meeting concluded with the selection of a committee which was to work for the thorough investigation of the sinkings, the location of the sunken vessels and the recovery of the bodies, the reimbursement to the captain-owner of the Marc Guylaine of his $50,000 down payment on the half-million dollar vessel, and the reimbursement of two-thirds of a regular season's wages to the captain and crew of the Marc Guylaine, who were unable to fish without the use of their vessel.

This committee was selected by the same procedure used earlier in the meeting. Individuals were nominated and seconded from the floor and elected by acclamation. Several individuals requested that their names be removed from nomination; all women who were nominated removed their names. There was no contesting of the appointments to the committee.

The committee comprised individuals who were formal leaders in the regional cooperatives, the president of the local fisherman's union, a fishing captain, and the brother of a fisherman lost in one sinking. Thus, no government figures or politicians, such as local mayors of Lameque or Shippegan town, were appointed to the committee. This is a common characteristic of "government by committee" in northeastern New Brunswick. Those who are elected to governing positions, such as that of mayor, are locally assumed to be biased towards their town or village. Their entrance to regional committees results in the belief that the committee work will not benefit the region as a whole, but will instead benefit only the home towns of the mayors. In the case of the Marc Guylaine there would have been little, if anything, to cause competition among committee members (e.g., press releases did not usually mention committee members by name and, hence, did not represent ways of providing the members with publicity and recognition); however, the pattern of not selecting town or village officials for regional committee posts was repeated. Instead, individuals were selected who are formal leaders in regional associations, e.g., the regional cooperatives, and who have no political advantages to give to one village over another. These regional voluntary associations provide a corpus of politically neutral and qualified people from whom members for committees and action groups are selected. The importance of these individuals in political and quasi-political activities in the area is considerable, though they hold no permanent political position.

The resulting committee in the Marc Guylaine affair held conferences with provincial and federal officials and generated much publicity, especially in the French-language communication media. Investigation of the seaworthiness of the Marc Guylaine was reopened, and the ship was ultimately condemned as unsafe. A financial settlement was made with the captain-owner of the Marc Guylaine; and, as predicted by local people, several of the survivors from the Lady Dorianne "lost their nerve" and no longer fish for a living.

The committee formed to work on the Marc Guylaine affair has not become embroiled in other issues affecting local fishermen, although members have individually become involved in such issues. The committee's function was to handle this one affair and with the achieving of goals, its reason for existence disappeared.

NOTES

PREFACE

1. When fieldwork was done, the island was known as Shippegan Island and on Map 1 is still so named. A few years later, the name was changed to Lameque Island, which I use in the text. The renaming reflects the islanders' wish that their island be seen as distinct from the mainland town of Shippegan. It does not reduce the confusion resulting from having the island carry the same name as a local village or town for the largest village on the island is also called Lameque.

Lameque and Miscou Islands and the immediately adjacent mainland, including Shippegan town, make up what I refer to as the Shippegan area. In recent government documents and in media communications, the place name "Acadian Peninsula" is often used; this refers to an area somewhat larger than that of Shippegan. The Acadian Peninsula is targeted for various government development projects, and the increased importance of cooperation within the region may serve to reduce old animosities between islanders and mainlanders.

Elsewhere I followed the convention of employing a pseudonym rather than the true name of the community studied, and I referred to the village as "St. Simon." However, anyone who knows the Shippegan area can readily identify "St. Simon" as Ste. Marie-sur-Mer. The coastal villages on Lameque Island are few, and there is only one with the geographical features of Ste. Marie. I could have created other geographical features and a new location for the village in an attempt to mask its identity, but other aspects of the description would have been made incongruous or would have been necessarily altered as well. Rather than following that undesireable course, I have used the name of the village here.

CANADIAN DUALISM AND THE ACADIAN DILEMMA

1. "An ethnic group is a distinct category of the population in a larger society whose culture is usually different from its own. The members of such a group are, or feel themselves, or are thought to be, bound together by common ties of race or nationality or culture" (Morris 1968:167).

2. Terms used to refer to French-speaking residents of Quebec take on political overtones, with French Canadian being supposedly used by those wishing Quebec to remain part of the Canadian federation and the term Quebecois being used by those wishing Quebec to become an independent nation (Rioux 1969).

3. According to 1981 census information, the percentage of francophones in Canada has dropped from 27 to 26 percent; however, in Quebec the percentage of francophones has increased from 80 to 82 percent. The over one-quarter million francophones in New Brunswick, representing 34 percent of the province, make up the largest francophone proportion of a provincial population outside of Quebec. The nearly half-million francophones in Ontario constitute only 6 percent of that province's population.

New Brunswick of all the provinces remains the most like Canada as a whole in its representation of francophones and anglophones. However, it exceeds Canada in being nearly exclusively composed of the two official language groups; only 1 percent of the population claim neither of the official languages as a mother tongue in comparison to the 13 percent who do so in Canada.

The number of bilingual speakers in Canada has increased in the period between 1971 and 1981; today about 15 percent of Canadians are bilingual in French and English. The proportions of bilingual speakers in Quebec and New Brunswick have also increased and remain the largest of provincial populations, 32 and 26 percent respectively. Ontario has over 900,000 bilinguals in French and English, but they represent only 11 percent of the province's population.

Francophones remain more apt than anglophones to become bilingual in French and English. Although only one indication of bilingualism and that most likely a result of marriages involving partners of different language backgrounds, nearly 10 percent of francophones in New Brunswick speak English at home, while only 2 percent of the province's anglophones speak French at home. In Canada the comparable figures indicate that 7 percent of francophones speak English at home, while less than 1 percent of anglophones speak the other official language at home (Statistics Canada 1984).

4. The last ten years have brought dramatic developments in Quebec. A series of Bills, most importantly Bill 22 (the Official Languages Act of 1974) and Bill 101 (the Charter of the French Language, passed in 1977), restricted the use of English and promoted the use of French in schools and the workplace. In 1976 the Parti Quebecois was elected to power; however, a 1980 referendum seeking Quebeckers' approval for the province's pursuit of separation from the federation was defeated. The Parti Quebecois, still in power, has reiterated that Quebec's separation from Canada remains its fundamental goal. However, support for the Parti Quebecois has sharply decreased most recently.

Wardhaugh's Language and Nationhood, The Canadian Experience (1983) provides a highly useful and readable account of these and other aspects of bilingualism and multiculturalism in Canada.

5. However, the political situation in New Brunswick has been suggested to be quite unlike that of Northern Ireland. The existence of cross-cutting ties between French and English in New Brunswick contributes to political stability, but in Northern Ireland, where such ties between Catholics and Protestants do not exist, political stability is absent (Aunger 1981).

6. French Canadians and English Canadians are often referred to as the two founding "races" in Canada; no biological meaning is attached to the usage of the term.

7. For a list of Research Reports submitted to the Royal Commission on Bilingualism and Biculturalism, see Royal Commission on Bilingualism and Biculturalism 1967:201-212.

8. The sociological and anthropological literature on French Canadians is growing, although studies of particular communities or regions are still limited. For examples of regional or community studies, see Gold (1975), Jackson (1975), Jaenen (1983), Juteau-Lee and Lapointe (1983), Waddell and Doran (1983).

9. The extent to which these disparities may have decreased represents a study in itself. However, the extensive information in the 1981 Census of Canada will allow at least some of the relevant comparisons to be made by future researchers.

10. The 1981 census information indicates that the predictions are being borne out. In New Brunswick's bilingual belt, one county (Victoria) increased slightly its percentage of francophones, three others (Westmoreland, Northumberland, and Restigouche) remained essentially the same, and three others (Kent, Madawaska and Gloucester) decreased slightly in the ten year period; the bilingual belt remains essentially intact. In Prince Edward Island and Nova Scotia, however, all counties in which francophones make up more than 10 percent of the population showed decreases ranging from 22 to 6 percent; the pockets of francophones have shrunk during the same period (see Table I).

ETHNIC RELATIONS, PERSISTENCE, AND ASSIMILATION: APPROACHES TO ACADIAN STUDIES

1. For an extensive bibliography of publications dealing with Acadians, see Tremblay 1962b; for a bibliography containing more recently published materials on Acadians and other French-speaking groups in Canada, see Research and Planning Branch (1972). See also the bibliographic sections regularly provided in the periodicals Canadian Historical Review, Acadiensis, and Société Historique Acadienne, Les cahiers.

2. The most noteworthy addition to the literature is The Acadians of the Maritimes (1982), edited by Jean Daigle. This volume contains survey articles and brief histories on various topics regarding Acadians.

3. The Société des Acadiens du Nouveau Brunswick (S.A.N.B.), the most important francophone lobbying group in the province, also sponsors research on a range of aspects of Acadian life, including language use and acculturation.

4. Richard and Hautecoeur have received training at Université de Laval in Quebec, where both prepared their theses in sociology (Hautecoeur 1971:272). Universities in Quebec were catalysts for social change in the 1960s. Intellectuals and students pushed for increased participation by all segments of the population in programs of change, especially those leading to the increased self-determination of the province (Rioux 1969). Social thought emanating from Quebec influenced francophone intellectuals elsewhere in Canada, and social action proposed among Acadians in New Brunswick appears to have parallels with that proposed earlier in Quebec.

A more recent example illustrates the same point. In 1979, at a time when Quebec independence was most discussed, a majority of delegates at the annual meeting of the S.A.N.B. approved the goal of a separate Acadian province. In 1984, after the defeat of the Quebec referendum and the lessening of the likelihood of Quebec separation, the idea of a separate Acadian province was not even discussed at the annual S.A.N.B. meeting.

5. The more recent strategy involves demands for the establishment of a structurally bilingual province; parallel economic, cultural, and social institutions, based in government services, would be provided anglophones and francophones. Services for the two language groups would be "separate, but equal." The provincial government has provided general support for this notion, as reflected in the passage in 1982 of further legislation regarding the use of the official languages.

6. The division did ultimately take place, but the Department of Education remains the only provincial department structurally divided in 1984.

7. In 1984, the Parti Acadien was no longer active, supporting the suggestion that the party had had no broadly based support in the Acadian community as a whole.

8. The S.A.N.B. is attempting to cope with the problem by establishing regional councils throughout the province to better attract participation at the grassroots level. Yet, in 1984 several of these councils were not functioning.

THE REGION

1. In 1981 the population in Shippegan Parish could still be described as under-educated; 53 percent of the adult population had achieved less than grade nine, the commonly accepted level of functional literacy (Statistics Canada 1984). Those who do not have grade nine or equivalent can be and often are denied entrance to government job training programs. During the last twenty years residents in Shippegan Parish have actually improved their overall educational levels very little in comparison to the increasing demands of the larger society.

MAKING A LIVING

1. This does not deny that in many cases income per capita or per household falls below what can be considered adequate, nor does this deny that many young educated villagers permanently leave the area in search of more profitable employment elsewhere. Upon leaving school, about five out of six villagers leave Ste. Marie to establish residence elsewhere.

PATTERNING CONTINUITY: KINSHIP

1. This figure is conservative in that genealogies were not traced out uniformly for all villagers; hence, there were undoubtedly relationships between marriage partners prior to their marriages which went undetected.

STRUCTURING INTERACTION: WITHIN THE PARISH

1. J. A. Barnes' distinction of three social fields -- industrial field, territorially-based field, and network -- has been modified here; I use "territorially-based field" to include administrative units (e.g., the parish), as does Barnes, and non-administrative units (e.g., the neighborhood and village), which Barnes does not do. I consider relationships enjoyed as householder, neighbor, and villager to be structured by the nature of the relevant territorial fields; however, Barnes would probably analyze these relationships within the context of "networks" (see Barnes 1954).

STRUCTURING INTERACTION: PARISH AND BEYOND

1. For further disucssion of language-based conflict in New Brunswick schools, see Sealy (1978).

POSTSCRIPT

1. The terms "middle distance or nearshore" fishery or mid-water fishery are relatively new. The latter fishery "emerged from the inshore fishery, with the acquisition by private fishermen of somewhat larger, more seaworthy and more sophisticated vessels. This allowed them to extend their range of operations as to distance travelled, numbers of days fished and variety of species caught, with consequent increases in annual catches obtainable per fisherman" (Copes 1978:160). Villagers earlier described as participating in the offshore fishery, i.e., those gone on fishing trips of two or three days at a time, would now be termed part of the mid-water fishery. Fishermen gone for weeks at a time or who fish on "factory" ships participate in the offshore fishery as it is more commonly referred to today. Less commonly do villagers work in this fishery.

2. A significant development in the inshore fishery was legislation passed which allows the Maritime Fishermen's Union to bargain collectively with the New Brunswick Fish Buyers Bargaining Association regarding prices for catches, including lobster. This may serve to increase prices to fishermen. However, in 1984 the buyers association was actually offering prices lower than in 1983.

This change also affects the nature of the fisherman-buyer relationship. If prices are common no matter the buyer, personal relationships may influence even more strongly a fisherman's choice of buyer.

3. Each fishery experiences different combinations of problems associated with market prices, quotas and resource management, the inefficient use of labor and capital, etc. There is no one set of problems or solutions applicable to all.

4. In 1981 there were 539 residents of Ste. Marie-sur-Mer (Statistics Canada 1984).

5. On the basis of past birth rates, I projected that village women married between 1960 and 1970 would have about half as many children as women married prior to 1940, or about five children per woman in comparison to the 10 children per woman in the preceding generation (Davis 1983:210). Recent census information on Shippegan Parish indicates that married women between the ages of 15 and 44 have on average two children, while those married women who are more than 45 years of age have averaged seven (Statistics Canada 1984).

BIBLIOGRAPHY

Adair, E. R.

    1954   French-Canadian seigneury. Canadian Historical Review 35:187-207.

Anderson, Raoul and Cato Wadel

    1972a   Introduction. In North Atlantic Fishermen, Anthropological Essays on Modern Fishing, Raoul Anderson and Cato Wadel, eds., Newfoundland Social and Economic Papers No. 5, St. John's, Institute of Social and Economic Research, Memorial University of Newfoundland.

    1972b   Comparative problems in fishing adaptations. In North Atlantic Fishermen, Anthropological Essays on Modern Fishing, Raoul Anderson and Cato Wadel, eds., Newfoundland Social and Economic Papers No. 5, St. John's, Institute of Social and Economic Research, Memorial University of Newfoundland.

Arsenault, Bona

    1966   History of the Acadians. Quebec, Le Conseil de la vie française en Amerique.

Aunger, Edmund A.

    1981   In Search of Political Stability, A Comparative Study of New Brunswick and Northern Ireland. Montreal, McGill-Queen's University Press.

Barnes, J. A.

    1954   Class and committees in a Norwegian island parish. Human Relations 7:39-58.

Barth, Frederik

    1966   Models of Social Organization, Occasional Paper No. 23. London, Royal Anthropological Society of Great Britain and Ireland.

Barth, Fredrik (cont.)

    1969a   Introduction. In Ethnic Groups and Boundaries, Fredrik Barth, ed., Boston, Little, Brown and Company.

    1969b   Pathan identity and its maintenance. In Ethnic Groups and Boundaries, Frederik Barth, ed., Boston, Little, Brown and Company.

Baudry, R.

    1966   Les Acadiens d'aujourd'hui. Rapport de recherche préparé pour la commission royale d'enquête sur le bilinguisme et le biculturalisme. Secrétariat d'État. microfilm.

Bird, J. B.

    1955   Settlement patterns in Maritime Canada, 1687-1786. Geographical Review 45:385-404.

Borhek, J. T.

    1970   Ethnic group cohesion. American Journal of Sociology 76:33-46.

Brent, Edmund

    1971   Canadian French: A Synthesis. Ph.D. dissertation, Cornell University.

Breton, Yvan

    1973   A comparative study of work groups in an eastern Canadian peasant community: bilateral kinship and adaptive processes. Ethnology 12:393-418.

Broom, Leonard

    1960   Urbanization and the plural society. In Social and Cultural Pluralism in the Caribbean, Vera Rubins, ed., Annals of the New York Academy of Sciences 83:761-916.

Cadieux, Jean

    1968   L'Acadie économique. La Revue de l'Université de Moncton 1:45-48.

Canada

    n.d.   Maps of Lameque Island and Gloucester County. Department of Energy, Mines, and Resources.

BIBLIOGRAPHY

Carisse, Colette

    1971   Cultural orientations in marriages between French and English Canadians. In Immigrant Groups, Jean Leonard Elliott, ed., Scarborough, Ontario, Prentice-Hall of Canada.

Charest, Paul

    n.d.   Cultural Ecology of the North Shore of the Gulf of St. Lawrence. MS. Department of Anthropology, University Laval.

Charron, J. P.

    1972   Costs and Earnings of Selected Fishing Enterprises, Atlantic Provinces. Primary Industry Studies, No. 1, Vol. 19. Social Science Research Branch, Fisheries and Marine Service, Environment Canada, Ottawa.

Chiasson, Père Anseleme

    1961   Chéticamp: Histoires et traditions acadiennes. Moncton, Nouveau-Brunswick, Éditions des Aboiteaux.

Clark, Barbara S.

    1971   Pre-school programs and black children. In Immigrant Groups, Jean Leonard Elliott, ed., Scarborough, Ontario, Prentice-Hall of Canada.

Comitas, Lambros

    1963   Occupational multiplicity in rural Jamaica. In Symposium on Community Studies in Anthropology, Viola E. Garfield, ed., Seattle, University of Washington Press.

Community Improvement Corporation Planning Department

    1968   Northeast New Brunswick, Outline Community Plans: Shippegan. Fredericton, N. B.

Cook, Ramsay

    1967   Canada and the French-Canadian Question. Toronto, Macmillan of Canada.

Copes, Parzival

    1978   Canada's Atlantic Coast fisheries: policy development and the impact of extended jurisdiction. Canadian Public Policy 4:155-171.

Copes, Parzival (cont.)

1979   The economics of marine fisheries management in the era of extended jurisdiction: the Canadian perspective. American Economic Review 69:256-260.

Daigle, Jean, ed.

1982   The Acadians of the Maritimes. Moncton, N.B. Centre d'études acadiennes, Université de Moncton.

Davis, Nanciellen

1981   Women's work and worth in an Acadian maritime village. In Women and World Change, Equity Issues in Development, Naomi Black and Ann Baker Cottrell, eds. Beverly Hills, Calif., Sage Publication, Inc.

1983   Acadian women: economic development, ethnicity and the status of women. In Two Nations, Many Cultures; Ethnic Groups in Canada (2nd Edition), Jean Leonard Elliott, ed. Scarborough, Ont., Prentice-Hall Canada Inc.

de la Garde, R.

1966   Utilisation de la langue française au Nouveau-Brunswick. Rapport de recherche préparé pour la commission royale d'enquête sur le bilinguisme et le biculturalisme. Secrétariat d'État. microfilm.

Denton, Trevor

1966   The structure of French Canadian acculturation, 1759-1800. Anthropologica 8:29-43.

Denys, Nicholas

1908   Description geographique et historique des côstes de l'Amerique septentrionale, trans. W. F. Ganong. Toronto, The Champlain Society.

Dugas, Eudore

1980   Operations of Selected Boats, New Brunswick North and Southeast Shores, 1979. Caraquet, N.B., Planning and Coordination, New Brunswick Department of Fisheries.

BIBLIOGRAPHY

Dulong, Gaston

    1961   Chéticamp, îlot linguistique du Cap-Breton. National Museum of Canada, Bulletin No. 173 Contributions to Anthropology. Ottawa.

Eidhem, Harald

    1969   When ethnic identity is a social stigma. In Ethnic Groups and Boundaries, Fredrik Barth, ed., Boston, Little, Brown and Company.

Elliott, Jean Leonard (ed.)

    1971   Immigrant Groups. Scarborough, Ontario, Prentice-Hall of Canada.

Environment Canada

    1973   Personal communication on inshore and offshore landings in New Brunswick fishing district #66, 1967-72. Marketing Services Branch. Ottawa.

Even, Alain

    1970   Le territoire pilote du Nouveau-Brunswick ou les blocages culturels au développement économique. Ph.D. dissertation, Rennes.

Falardeau, Jean-Charles

    1949   The parish as an institutional type. Canadian Journal of Economics and Political Science 15:353-67.

Faris, James C.

    1966   Cat Harbour: a Newfoundland Fishing Settlement. Newfoundland Social and Economic Studies No. 3, St. John's, Institute of Social and Economic Research, Memorial University of Newfoundland.

Firestone, Melvin

    1967   Brothers and Rivals: Patrilocality in Savage Cove. Newfoundland Social and Economic Studies No. 5, St. John's, Institute of Social and Economic Research, Memorial University of Newfoundland.

Fortin, Gérald

    1968   Socio-cultural changes in an agricultural parish. In French-Canadian Society, Volume I,

Fortin, Gérald (cont.)

> Marcel Rioux and Yves Martin, eds., The Carleton Library No. 18, Toronto, McClelland and Stewart Limited.

Gallagher, D. W.

1955   The Commercial Fisheries of New Brunswick, 1926-53. M.A. thesis, University of New Brunswick, Fredericton.

Ganong, W. F.

1906   The history of Miscou. Acadiensis 6:79-94.

1908   The history of Shippegan. Acadiensis 8:138-61.

Garigue, Phillipe

1958   Change and continuity in rural French Canada. In Études sur le Canada français, Phillipe Garigue, ed., Montreal, Faculté des Sciences Sociales Economiques et Politiques, Université des Montreal.

Garner, John

1953   The enfrancisement of Roman Catholics in the Maritimes. Canadian Historical Review 34: 203-18.

Gold, Gerald L.

1975   St. Pascal, Changing Leadership & Social Organization in a Quebec Town. Toronto, Holt, Rinehart & Winston of Canada, Limited.

Gordon, Milton M.

1964   Assimilation in American Life. New York, Oxford University Press.

Hautecoeur, Jean-Paul

1971   Variations et invariance de l'Acadie dans le néo-nationalisme. Recherches Sociographiques 12:259-70.

Hebert, Raymond and Jean-Guy Vaillancourt

1971   French-Canadians in Manitoba: elites and ideologies. In Immigrant Groups, Jean Leonard Elliott, ed., Scarborough, Ontario, Prentice-Hall of Canada.

BIBLIOGRAPHY

Henripin, J.

    1966   Étude demographique des groupes ethniques et linguistiques au Canada. Rapport de recherche préparé pour la commission royale d'enquête sur le bilingisme et le biculturalisme. Secrétariat d'État. microfilm.

Henry, Frances

    1973   Forgotten Canadians: The Blacks of Nova Scotia, Don Mills, Ontario, Longman Canada Limited.

Hughes, Charles C., Marc-Adèlard Tremblay, Robert N. Rapoport, and Alexander H. Leighton

    1960   People of Cove and Woodlot. New York, Basic Books.

Innis, H. A.

    1940   The Cod Fisheries: The History of an International Economy. New Haven, Yale University Press.

Jackson, John D.

    1975   Community and Conflict: A Study of French-English Relations in Ontario. Toronto, Holt, Rinehart and Winston of Canada, Limited.

Jaenen, Cornelius J.

    1983   French roots in the Prairies. In Two Nations, Many Cultures, Jean Leonard Elliott, ed. Scarborough, Ontario, Prentice-Hall Canada, Inc.

Jolicoeur, G.

    1966   L'acculturation chez les Canadiens Français du Manitoba. Rapport de recherche préparé pour la commission royale d'enquête sur le bilinguisme et le biculturalisme. Secrétariat d'État. microfilm.

Joy, Richard J.

    1972   Languages in Conflict: the Canadian Experience. The Carleton Library No. 61, Toronto, McClelland and Stewart Limited, First Published by the Author, 1967.

Joy, Richard J. (cont.d)

1976 Languages in conflict: Canada, 1976. American Review of Canadian Studies VI (2):7-21.

Junek, O. W.

1937 Isolated Communities: A Study of a Labrador Fishing Village. Germany, American Book Company.

Juteau-Lee, Danielle and Jean Lapointe

1983 From French Canadians to Franco-Ontarians and Ontarois: New boundaries, new identities. In Two Nations, Many Cultures, Jean Leonard Elliott, ed. Scarborough, Ontario, Prentice-Hall Canada, Inc.

Keesing, Roger M. and Felix M. Keesing

1971 New Perspectives in Cultural Anthropology. New York, Holt, Rinehart and Winston.

Lamarre, Nicolle

1971 Parenté et héritage du patrimoine dans un village français terre-neuvien. Recherches Sociographiques 12:344-59.

LeBlanc, Robert G.

1970 The Acadian migrations. Canadian Geographical Journal 81:11-19.

Lieberson, Stanley

1970 Language and Ethnic Relations in Canada. New York, John Wiley and Sons.

MacNutt, W. S.

1965 The Atlantic Provinces, The Emergence of Colonial Society, 1712-1857. Toronto, McClelland and Stewart Limited.

Maheu, Robert

1970 Les Francophones du Canada, 1941-1991. Montreal, les Éditions Parti-Pris.

Massignon, Genevieve

1962   Les Parlers francais d'Acadie; enquête linguistique. Paris, Libraire, C. Klinchsieck.

Michaud, Marguerite

1955   La reconstruction française au Nouveau Brunswick, Buctouche, paroisse-type. Fredericton, Les Presses Universitaires.

Michelson, William

1971   Some like it hot: social participation and environmental use as functions of the season. American Journal of Sociology 74:1072-83.

Miner, Horace

1967   St. Denis, A French-Canadian Parish. Chicago, University of Chicago Press, Phoenix Books.

Mitchell, C. L.

1978   The 200-mile limit: new issues, old problems for Canada's East Coast fisheries. Public Policy 4 (2):172-183.

Morris, H. S.

1968   Ethnic groups. International Encyclopedia of the Social Sciences Volume 5:167-172, David L. Sills, ed., Macmillan and Company and the Free Press.

Nemec, Thomas F.

1972   I fish with my brother: the structure and behavior of agnatic-based fishing crews in a Newfoundland Irish outport. In North Atlantic Fishermen, Anthropological Essays on Modern Fishing, Raoul Anderson and Cato Wadel, eds., Newfoundland Social and Economic Papers No. 5, St. John's Institute of Social and Economic Research, Memorial University of Newfoundland.

Opler, Morris E.

1956   The extensions in an Indian Village. Journal of Asian Studies 16:5-10.

Perley, M. G., Esquire

    1852   Reports on the Sea and River Fisheries of New Brunswick. Fredericton, Printer to the Queen.

Piddington, Ralph

    1965   Kinship network among French Canadians. International Journal of Comparative Sociology 6: 145-65.

Poulin, Pierre

    1972   L'Acadien à la recherche d'une Acadie. Relations 371:135-138.

Prattis, J. I.

    1981   The author's ideology: a dilemma for maritime studies. Economic Development and Cultural Change 30: 183-192.

Putnam, Donald F.

    1940   The climate of the Maritime Provinces. Canadian Geographical Journal 20/21:134-47.

    1952   Canadian Regions; A Geography of Canada. Toronto, J. M. Dent and Sons, Limited.

Raîche, Victor

    1962   La population du nord et de l'est du Nouveau Brunswick et son milieu géographique. M.A. thesis, Université d'Ottawa.

Research and Planning Branch

    1972   Selected Bibliography on Francophone Minorities in Canada, Parts I and II. Bilingualism Development Programme, Department of the Secretary of State, Ottawa.

Richard, Camille

    1969   L'Acadie, une histoire à faire? Maintenant 87: 169-75.

Richer, Stephen, and Pierre Laporte

    1971   Culture, cognition and English-French competition. In Immigrant Groups, Jean Leonard Elliott, ed., Scarborough, Ontario, Prentice-Hall of Canada.

Rioux, Marcel

 1955/56 Rapport préliminaire de l'étude sur la culture acadienne du Nouveau Brunswick. Extrait du Bulletin No. 147. Rapport annuel du Musée National, Ministère du Nord Canadien et des Resources Nationales, Ottawa.

 1959 Kinship recognition and urbanization in French Canada. National Museum of Canada, Bulletin No. 173, Contributions to Anthropology, Ottawa.

 1969 Quebec: from a minority complex to majority behavior. In Minorities and Politics, Henry J. Tobias and Charles E. Woodhouse, eds., Albuquerque, University of New Mexico.

Royal Commission on Bilingualism and Biculturalism

 1967 Report, Book I: The Official Languages. Ottawa, The Queen's Printer.

Rudie, Ingrid

 1969/70 Household organization: adaptive process and restrictive form, a viewpoint on economic change. Folk 11/12:185-200.

Runciman, W. G.

 1969 The three dimensions of social inequality. In Social Inequality, Andre Beteille, ed. England, Penguin Education.

Savoie, Francis

 1967 L'île de Shippegan, anecdotes, tours et légendes. Moncton, N. B., Éditions des Aboiteaux.

Schneider, David M.

 1968 American Kinship: A Cultural Account. Englewood Cliffs, New Jersey, Prentice-Hall.

Sealy, Nanciellen Davis

 1977 Diverse perspectives dans l'étude de la survivance du groupe ethnique acadien. Société Historique Acadienne, Les cahiers 8 (2):53-64.

 1978 Language conflict and schools in New Brunswick. In Ethnic Canadians: Culture and Education, Martin L. Kovac, ed. Regina, Sask., Canadian Plains Research Centre, University of Regina.

Smith, Robert J., and Eudaldo P. Reyes

    1957   Community interrelations with the outside world; the case of a Japanese agricultural community. American Anthropologist 59:463-72.

Société D'Aménagement Régional Service D'Urbanisme

    1968   Le nord-est du Nouveau-Brunswick, plan d'urbanisme, Rapport Préliminaire, Étude: Vieme Parti, Shippegan. Fredericton.

Statistics Canada

    1973   Census of Canada, 1971. Ottawa.

    1984   Census of Canada, 1981. Ottawa.

Stiles, R. Geoffrey

    1972   Fishermen, wives and radios: aspects of communication in a Newfoundland fishing community. In North Atlantic Fishermen, Anthropological Essays on Modern Fishing, Raoul Anderson and Cato Wadel, eds., Newfoundland Social and Economic Papers No. 5, St. John's, Institute of Social and Economic Research, Memorial University of Newfoundland.

Szwed, John

    1966   Private Cultures and Public Imagery: Interpersonal Relations in a Newfoundland Peasant Society. Newfoundland Social and Economic Studies No. 2, St. John's Institute of Social and Economic Research, Memorial University of Newfoundland.

Thorburn, H. G.

    1961   Politics in New Brunswick. Toronto, University of Toronto Press.

    1971   French in the New Brunswick civil service: ethnic participation and language use. Canadian Ethnic Studies 3:23-54.

Tremblay, Marc-Adélard

    1961   Niveaux et dynamismes d'acculturation des Acadiens de Portsmouth. Anthropologica 3: 303-51.

Tremblay, Marc-Adélard (cont.)

    1962a   Le transfert culturel: fondement et extension dans le processus d'acculturation. Anthropologica 4:293-320.

    1962b   L'état des recherches sur la culture acadienne. Recherches Sociographiques 3:145-70.

    1966   La société acadienne en devenir: l'impact de la technique sur la structure sociale global. Anthropologica 8:329-50.

    1971   Famille et Parenté en Acadie. National Museum of Man, Publications in Ethnology, No. 3, Ottawa.

Vallee, Frank G.

    1969   The viability of French groupings outside of Quebec. In Regionalism in the Canadian Community, Mason Wade ed., Toronto, University of Toronto.

    1971   Regionalism and ethnicity: the French Canadian case. In Immigrant Groups, Jean Leonard Elliott, ed., Scarborough, Ontario, Prentice-Hall of Canada.

Vallee, Frank G., Mildred Schwartz, and Frank Darknell

    1971   Ethnic assimilation and differentiation in Canada. In Canadian Society, Sociological Perspectives, Bernard R. Blishen et al., eds., (abridged edition), Toronto, MacMillan of Canada.

van den Berghe, Pierre

    1970   Ethnic membership and cultural change in Guatemala. In Race and Ethnicity, Pierre L. van den Berghe, ed., New York, Basic Books, Inc.

Waddell Eric and Claire Doran

    1983   "The Newfoundland French: an endangered minority?" In Two Nations, Many Cultures, Jean Leonard Elliott, ed. Scarborough, Ontario, Prentice-Hall Canada, Inc.

Wade, Mason (ed.)

    1960   Canadian Dualism, Studies of French-English Relations. Toronto, University of Toronto Press.

Wade, Mason

    1962   Two French Canadas: Quebec and Acadia. In French Canada Today, F. F. MacRae, ed., Mount Allison University Publication No. 6, Sackville, N. B., Mount Allison University.

Wadel, Cato

    1969   Marginal Adaptations and Modernization in Newfoundland, A Study of Strategies and Implications in the Resettlement and Redevelopment of Outport Fishing Communities. Newfoundland Social and Economic Studies No. 7, St. John's, Institute of Social and Economic Research, Memorial University of Newfoundland.

Wagley, Charles, and Marvin Harris

    1967   The French Canadians. In Minorities in the New World, Charles Wagley and Marvin Harris, eds., New York, Columbia University Press, Columbia Paperback Edition.

Wardhaugh, Ronald

    1983   Language and Nationhood, the Canadian Experience. Vancouver, New Star Books.

Whitten, Norman E., Jr.

    1970   Network analysis in Equador and Nova Scotia; some critical remarks. Canadian Review of Sociology and Anthropology 7:269-80.

Wylie, Laurence

    1964   Village in the Vaucluse. New York, Harper and Row, Publishers, First Harper Colophon Edition.

INDEX

Acadia (French colony). See New France

Acadian ethnicity: French language and, 164, 165-166, 173; historical origins and, 164-165, 172; residence in Maritime Provinces and, 164; Roman Catholicism and, 164, 172-174

Acadian Peninsula. See New Brunswick, Northeastern

Acadians, 1, 2, 6, 12 (defined), 14-18; adherence to Catholic faith, 30-31, 164; anthropological studies of, 20, 26-27; church affairs of, 153; economic adaptation of, 91-92; grand dérangement of, 14-15, 19, 26, 42-44, 53, 128, 165, 172; in government, 152; in Nova Scotia, 27-28, 31; intermarriage of, 118; origins of, 14; patriotic groups among, 153; poverty among, 22-23, 47-48; relations with Anglo-Canadians, 1, 14, 21-23, 24, 25, 26, 27, 31, 36-37, 45, 66, 76, 78, 79, 93, 118-122, 143, 164, 175; renaissance acadienne, 19, 28; resistance to acculturation and assimilation of, 22, 24, 25, 36, 158; social groupings, 124-143. See also Acadian ethnicity; Sainte Marie-sur-Mer: Acadian life style of; Société des Acadiens du Nouveau-Brunswick

Acculturation, 2-3, 5, 6, 17-18, 19, 21, 22, 24, 25, 27, 29-31, 36, 46, 53, 92, 94. See also Ethnic persistence

Agricultural Rehabilitation and Development Act (1962), 21

Anderson, Raoul, cited, 76, 77, 87

Anglo-Canadians, 1, 2, 4 (defined), 8-9, 14; monolingualism of, 153. See also Acadians: relations with Anglo-Canadians

Anse des Lavallée, 28, 29

Arsenault, Bona, cited, 12, 14, 43

Assimilation, 2-3; behavioral assimilation, <u>see</u> Acculturation; structural assimilation, 3, 6, 29, 31, 32

Association Coopérative des Pêcheurs de l'Île, 79-80

Aunger, Edmund A., cited, 9 n

Barnes, J. A., cited, 86, 124 n, 148

Barth, Frederik, cited, 1, 35, 37, 84, 159, 161-162, 162-164, 165, 171, 176

Bathurst, 40, 46, 49, 50-51, 52, 149, 150

Baudry, R., cited, 21, 22, 23, 40, 44, 46, 48

Bilingualism, 4 (defined), 5-10, 36-37, 83-84, 94, 151-155, 168, 170, 185; and education, 153-154; of government representatives, 150-151; of native French speakers, 152-153. <u>See</u> <u>also</u> Royal Commission on Bilingualism and Biculturalism

Bird, J. B., cited, 42

Blanc Sablon, 83-84

Boats, types of, 69, 72. See also <u>Marc Guylaine</u> affair

Borhek, J. T., cited, 2

Brent, Edmund, cited, 15, 21

Breton, Yvan, cited, 76

Broom, Leonard, cited, 7

Cadieux, Jean, cited, 22, 24

Canada (French colony). <u>See</u> New France

Caraquet, 72, 74, 78, 79, 184; School of Fisheries, 74

Carisse, Colette, cited, 94

Cartier, Jacques, 41

INDEX

Chambre de Commerce, 34, 104, 125, 145, 146, 147, 149

Charest, Paul, cited, 11, 76

Charron, J. P., cited, 74, 179

Chiasson, Père Anselme, cited, 20

Chiasson Office, 55

Clark, Barbara S., cited, 20

Club Richelieu, 34

Comitas, Lambros, cited, 89, 90, 91

Community closure. See Institutional completeness

Community Improvement Corporation Planning Dept., cited, 21, 46-47, 51

Conseil Régionale Area Nord-Est (C.R.A.N.), 148-149

Contacts, structure of, defined, 36

Cook, Ramsay, cited, 6

Copes, Parzival, cited, 178, 179 n

Credit union, 80, 125-126, 136, 145, 146

Daigle, Jean, cited, 21 n

Darknell, Frank, cited, 3

Davis, Nanciellen, cited, 176, 182, 187 n

de la Garde, R., cited, 11, 14, 21

Denton, Trevor, cited, 6, 14, 37

Denys, Nicholas, 42

Doran, Claire, cited, 11 n

Dugas, Eudore, cited, 179

Dulong, Gaston, cited, 20

Environment Canada, cited, 74

Ethnic persistence, 1, 2, 3, 5, 6, 11, 17-18, 19, 25, 29, 31, 36, 37, 45, 53, 158-175; and exclusion, 159-162; religion and, 169; residence and, 169. See also Language retention

Évangéline (newspaper), 49, 166, 184

Evangeline (poem), 15

Even, Alain, cited, 24, 25, 39

Fabrique (church committee), 131, 141

Falardeau, Jean-Charles, cited, 169

Famille, 95 (defined), 96-105; parents and children in, 96-98; sexual division of labor in, 103-104; siblings in, 98-101; spouses in, 101-105

Faris, James C., cited, 20, 76, 128

Farming, 61, 88

Firestone, Melvin, cited, 20, 76

Fishing, 40-41, 46, 60-61, 66-84, 177-181; "banks", 41; broker-fishermen and, 79-84; cooperative, 79-80, 81; crews, 76-79; 200-mile limit and, 178. See also Marc Guylaine affair; Sainte Marie-sur-Mer: economic activities; Sainte Marie-sur-Mer: fishery

Fortin, Gérald, cited, 126

Gallagher, D. W., cited, 88

Ganong, W. F., cited, 20, 42

Garner, John, cited, 173

Gold, Gerald L., cited, 11 n

Gordon, Milton M., cited, 2-3, 5, 22

Grand dérangement. See: Acadians: grand dérangement of

INDEX

Harris, Marvin, cited, 6, 9-10

Hautecoeur, Jean-Paul, cited, 24, 25

Hebert, Raymond, cited, 11

Henripin, J., cited, 11

Henry, Frances, cited, 20

Household, 107-123, 124, 143; contemporary, 110-111; incomes, 133; mate selection and, 114-123; neighborhood and, 124-125; in recent past, 108-110; selection of, 114-123. *See also* Sainte Marie-sur-Mer: households

Hudson Bay Company, 84

Hughes, Charles C., cited, 15, 29, 30

Innis, H. A., cited, 83

Institutional completeness, 31-32 (defined), 35, 158, 161

Jackson, John D., cited, 11 n

Jaenen, Cornelius J., cited, 11 n

Jolicoeur, G., cited, 11

Joy, Richard J., cited, 11, 17, 30, 36

Junek, O. W., cited, 84

Juteau-Lee, Danielle, cited, 11 n

Keesing, Felix M, cited, 16

Keesing, Roger M., cited, 16

Kinship, 94-123; See also *Famille*; Household; Neighborhood; *Parenté*

Lameque (town), 38, 49, 51, 64, 72, 79, 85

Lameque Island, 38-39, 41, 42, 47, 50, 52, 55, 68, 83, 84, 85, 115-116, 149, 203

Language adoption, defined, 4

Language retention, 36, 37, 158

Language rights, 3, 7-9, 16, 166, 173

Lapointe, Jean, cited, 11 n

LeBlanc, Robert G., cited, 43

Leighton, Alexander H., cited, 15, 29, 30

Liberal Party, 146-147

Lieberson, Stanley, cited, 11, 17

Liturgical calendar, influence of, 63-64, 65

Loggie, W. S., Company, Ltd., 79-80, 81-84, 85; as an Anglo-Canadian enterprise, 81-82

Longfellow, Henry Wadsworth, 15

Lumbering, 88

MacNutt, W. S., cited, 172

Madawaska, Republic de, 28

Maheu, Robert, cited, 11, 17

Marc Guylaine affair, 149-150, 176, 194-202

Maritime communities, features common to, 87

Maritime Provinces, 11-12, 19, 21, 24, 29

Maritime Union, 24

Marriage, 114-123; and religion, 118-119, 120-121

Massignon, Genevieve, cited, 21

Michaud, Marguerite, cited, 20

Michelson, William, cited, 62

Micmac Indians, 42

Miner, Horace, cited, 20

Miscou Island, 41, 42, 50, 79, 83, 84, 85; Anglo-Canadian residents of, 119-120

Mitchell, C. L., cited, 178

Moncton, 28, 34, 49, 166, 168, 169, 171, 183, 184; Université de, 26, 52

Morris, H. S., cited, 2 n, 134

Neighborhood, as social unit, 124-125, 143

Nemec, Thomas F., cited, 76

New Brunswick: Acadian society in, 27, 28, 33, 183-184, 186-187; Catholic Church in, 153; class differences in, 175; divisions within Acadian population of, 183-184, 186-187; ethnic boundaries of, 171-175; francophone institutions of, 33-35; francophone populations of, 27-28, 32, 33-34; industrialization of, 25; language switching in, 168; Liberal Party in, 146-147; Northeastern, see New Brunswick, Northeastern; Official Languages Act, 8; politics in, 152; provincial government of, 154; settlement of, 12, 20, 41-44; socioeconomic position of Acadians in, 22, 24, 25, 26

New Brunswick, Northeastern: Anglo fishing interests in, 83, 84; communication and transportation in, 49-50; depressed economy of, 89, 92-93, 177, 178, 181-182; economy of, 46-48; fishing resources of, 40-41, 46, 88, 177-181; government intervention in, 177-179; history of, 41-46; physical geography of, 39-41; regional citizens' groups in, 148; service centers of, 50-53; signs of prosperity in, 181; social welfare in, 47-48. See also: Acadians

New France, 6, 12, 14, 42-43

Occupational plurality, defined, 89

Official Languages Act of 1969, 7-8

Parenté, 95 (defined), 105-107, 117

Parish, as unit of social organization, 15, 125-126, 135-143, 144-149, 169. See also Saint Raphael Parish

Parish Committee, 139-141

Parish priest, 132, 136, 140, 141-143

Parti Acadien, 34, 34 n, 146

Parti Quebecois, 9

Peat moss plants, 46, 47

Perley, M. G., cited, 83, 131

Poulin, Pierre, cited, 24, 25, 26, 33

Prattis, J. I., cited, 178

Putnam, Donald F., cited, 40

Quebecker, 4 (defined), 4 n, 7, 9, 12, 14, 16-17, 18; differences between Acadians and, 14-17, 26, 32-33, 122

Raîche, Victor, cited, 46

Rang (parish division), 126

Rapoport, Robert N., cited, 15, 29, 30

Research and Planning Branch, cited, 19 n

Richard, Camille, cited, 24, 25, 26

Rioux, Marcel, cited, 4 n, 9, 24 n, 28

Royal Commission on Bilingualism and Biculturalism, cited, 4, 5, 6, 7, 8, 11, 11 n, 21-22, 30

Rudie, Ingrid, cited, 87

INDEX

Runciman, W. G., cited, 182

Rural Economic Development Act (1966), 21

Sagouine, La, 17

Saint Raphael Parish, 55, 62, 77, 126, 135-143; governing committees of, 148; Parish Committee of, 139-141; parish priest of, 141-143; as religious field, 136-139; as social field, 139-143

Saint Raphael-sur-Mer, 56, 58, 59

Sainte Julienne, 126

Sainte Marie-sur-Mer: 1, 12, 55-65; Acadian dialect in, 166; Acadian life style of, 167-171; age distribution in, 39; and bilingualism, 151-155, 170; bridge to mainland from, 116; characteristics of interpersonal relationships in, 128-135; contacts with Anglophone world, 155-157; economic activities, see Sainte Marie-sur-Mer, economic activities of; elections, 146; fishery, 39, 60-61, 66-84, 177-181, 187; government representatives and, 150-151; households, 59-60 (see also household); intermediaries with government, 144-155; Marc Guylaine affair and, 149-150; neighborhoods, 57-60; parish associations, 145-149; representative of northeastern New Brunswick, 38; seasons, influence of, 61-63, 65, 68; settlement pattern of, 56-57; shopping in, 58-59; social and recreational activities, 62-65; social groupings, 124-143 (see also household; parish; village); special action groups in, 149-150; strangers in, 128-130; as unincorporated village, 145; wharf in, 136

Sainte Marie-sur-Mer, economic activities of: 60-62, 66-93; credit unions, 80; economic adaptation, 87-91; economic diversity, 87-91; economic relationships and social life, 86-87; income differences, 186-187; inshore fishery, 68-71, 77, 79, 88; locally owned enterprises, 85-86; multiple incomes, 182; offshore fishery, 71-76, 77, 78, 79, 88; usines, 85 (see also usines); work cycles, 68, 75-76

Savoie, Francis, cited, 21

Schneider, David M., cited, 95

Schwartz, Mildred, cited, 3

Sealy, Nanciellen Davis, cited, 154 n

Shippegan (town), 51, 52, 53, 72, 85, 116

Shippegan area, defined, 203. See also New Brunswick, Northeastern

Shippegan Island. See Lameque Island

Social units. See Household; Parish; Village

Société d'Aménagement Régional, Service d'Urbanisme, cited, 48

Société de la Mutual Assomption, 34

Société des Acadiens du Nouveau-Brunswick (S.A.N.B.), 22 n, 24 n, 25, 34, 34 n, 153, 184, 186

Statistics Canada, cited, 39, 47-48, 152, 181, 181 n, 182

Stiles, R. Geoffrey, cited, 112

Stirling County Study, 29

Szwed, John, cited, 20

Thorburn, H. G., cited, 45, 153, 154, 173

Treaty of Paris (1763), 43, 172

Tremblay, Marc-Adèlard, cited, 15, 19 n, 20, 28, 29-30, 31, 92, 94, 170

Usines (fish processing plants), 46-47, 66, 72, 79-81, 85, 177, 180, 181, 182

Vaillancourt, Jean-Guy, cited, 11

Vallee, Frank G., cited, 3, 31-32, 33, 34-35, 36, 158, 170

van den Berghe, Pierre, cited, 168

Village, as social unit, 125-135, 143

INDEX

Waddell, Eric, cited, 11 n
Wade, Mason, cited, 11, 14, 16
Wadel, Cato, cited, 20, 76, 77, 87
Wagley, Charles, cited, 6, 9-10
Wardhaugh, Ronald cited, 9 n, 185
Whitten, Norman E., Jr., cited, 20

WHITMAN COLLEGE LIBRARY

WITHDRAWN BY
WHITMAN COLLEGE LIBRARY

DATE DUE

DEMCO 38-297